TOURNAMENT WEEK

Also by John Strege

Off the Record
Tiger

TOURNAMENT WEEK

INSIDE THE ROPES
AND BEHIND THE SCENES
ON THE PGA TOUR

JOHN STREGE

Cliff Street Books
An Imprint of HarperCollins*Publishers*

HarperCollins books may be purchased for educational, business, or sales promotional use. For information please write: Special Markets Department, HarperCollins Publishers Inc., 10 East 53rd Street, New York, NY 10022.

FIRST EDITION

Printed on acid-free paper

Designed by William Ruoto

Library of Congress Cataloging-in-Publication Data has been applied for.

ISBN 0-06-019669-6

00 01 02 03 04 ❖/HC 10 9 8 7 6 5 4 3 2 1

For Hannah
A godsend

CONTENTS

ACKNOWLEDGMENTS

This was an undertaking that would have stalled at the outset without the support and effort of a very special person. I wish to thank my wife, Marlene, for the sacrifices she made, which were greater than my own.

I am indebted to Larry Dorman, for his unceasing support, as well as for his contributions to this project, and to Robinson Holloway, for her assistance on research.

I wish to acknowledge the best group of magazine editors in the business, foremost among them Jerry Tarde, as well as those with whom I work most closely: Roger Schiffman, Mike O'Malley, Peter McCleery, Peter Farricker, Terry Galvin, Geoff Russell, Ron Sirak, John Hawkins, Tim Murphy, and Alan Pittman. I would be remiss in not acknowledging Nick Seitz as well.

For inspiration and moral support, I turned to my friends Loree and Michael, Grace, Marilyn, Christina, Joseph, and Sarah, as well as my parents, Dorothy and Bill Strege, and I thank them all. Thank you, too, to my friend Jo Ann Rossi, for her efforts on my behalf.

Thanks to all who contributed to this project, including the PGA Tour players who agreed to share anecdotes, and to Steve Mata, Mike Galeski, Greg McLaughlin, and my colleagues in the press room who lent assists, including Thomas Bonk, Melanie Hauser, Bob Harig, Glenn Sheeley, and Mark Soltau.

I was exceedingly fortunate to have the opportunity to work on this project with a brilliant editor, Diane Reverand.

Finally, to my agent and friend, Freya Manston, whose powers of persuasion know no bounds, where would I be without you?

INTRODUCTION

When the legendary Bobby Jones saw Jack Nicklaus play golf for the first time, he observed a man playing a game with which he was not familiar. What then could the rest of us have known? For that matter, what do we know about the game at large, as it is played on the PGA Tour, even by those with no grip on immortality?

Professional golf is said to be among the most intimate of sports. Only a thin rope separates the players from the fans. Yet the reality is that the rope is a substantial barrier that permits only a glimpse of a world of which anyone who has ever played through the dew at sunrise has longed to be a part. What, we ask wistfully, is it like to play professional tournament golf at its highest level?

Forty-nine tournaments make up the PGA Tour, which starts in January and ends in November and circumnavigates the United States and beyond. We are told that there are four major championships—the Masters, the U.S. Open, the British Open, and the PGA Championship. A de facto fifth major, its relative unimportance notwithstanding, is the tournament that comes to your hometown once a year. It might lack the cachet of the Masters or the Open. The strength of its field might be a fraction of that for the PGA Championship. But for those from the community in which it is played, it feels very much like a major, beginning with the gentle buzz it creates on Monday of tournament week to the screeching crescendo it reaches on Sunday.

Typically fans are provided only a superficial glimpse. They see manicured fairways and perfect greens and conclude that PGA Tour players are pampered, but the degree to which they are coddled goes largely unseen.

"Life is so different here," said the Frenchman Jean Van de Velde, who chose to join the PGA Tour in 2000. "They treat you like royalty. Everything is designed to make things easy. Look at your highways. Four lanes on each side. It's a shame you can only go fifty-five."

What's the rush? Tempo is the cornerstone of a good golf swing, which begins deliberately and gradually gathers momentum, finally delivering a crushing blow. Tournament week follows a similar pattern.

The Tuesday practice round is a low-key though often highly competitive affair, to which the public is not privy. Players routinely play for their own money on this day, though the ultimate prize for which they are playing is pride.

The Wednesday pro-am unites the professionals with their constituency, amateur golfers paying for the privilege of venturing inside the ropes and exhibiting eyesore swings that endanger those outside the ropes.

Smiles have faded by Thursday morning, when the tournament begins. Stakes are high; in 2000, the PGA Tour will pay out $157 million in prize money. The winner each week receives eighteen percent of the total purse. A $3 million tournament, for instance, awards $560,000 to the winner. The cost of a solitary misguided stroke can be substantial. Matt Gogel, a rookie on the PGA Tour, missed a simple two-foot par putt on the last hole of the AT&T Pebble Beach National Pro-Am, dropping from sole possession of second place into a second-place tie. The difference in money was $80,000, a steep price to pay for a moment of carelessness.

Each day of tournament week, the pressure increases exponentially, finally peaking on Sunday, the defining day of a career, when the manner in which players respond is the device by which their talent ultimately is measured. Marshals hoist signs that ask for "Quiet Please," and by Sunday afternoon the silence is deafening.

This is the moment when those who summon equal measures of fortitude and skill venture fearlessly into the snake pit and emerge unscathed, trophy in tow, heroic survivors of this exercise in perseverance, this journey across the manicured landscape known as tournament week.

1

WALL-TO-WALL RED CARPET

A rusty nail on a back-room wall was tantamount to a locker in the early days of the PGA Tour. Players were unwelcome in the club-house, even the flamboyant Walter Hagen, who knew how to make an entrance and was determined to do so in this case. The pro who once arrived on the first tee attired in last night's tuxedo was said to have brazenly walked through the clubhouse doors, effectively opening them in perpetuity for his professional brethren.

Today's players walk through them and into a world of opulence. The life of a PGA Tour professional is a frill a minute, the red carpet extending wall to wall, inside or outside the clubhouse. Need a car? Here are the keys. Tickets to the Cubs? At will call. Phone service? In the clubhouse. Shoes shined, laundry done, dinner reservations, a massage? At your service.

The perk is part of the mating ritual, the persistent wooing of players by tournament directors attempting to bolster their marquee. Offer the players the world, and they might agree to visit your small corner of it.

This is where tournament week begins, and it does not necessarily begin on Monday, a fact to which Greg McLaughlin readily could attest. McLaughlin, the tournament director of the Advil (formerly Motorola) Western Open, once held a similar post with the Nissan Los Angeles Open. In 1992, he extended a sponsor's exemption to a sixteen-year-old amateur who was precocious, though not yet a bona fide gate attraction. Tiger Woods gratefully accepted. The following year, when McLaughlin was directing the Honda Classic in Ft. Lauderdale, Florida, he again extended a sponsor's exemption to Woods, then seventeen, and paired him in the pro-am with a foursome of star quarterbacks from the National Football League: Dan Marino, Phil Simms, Bernie Kosar, and Mark Rypien.

The courtesy McLaughlin demonstrated toward Woods and his family during those two tournaments made a lasting impression that continues to pay dividends. Woods has played in the Western Open in each of his three full seasons as a professional and has won the event twice. "Greg McLaughlin is one of my great friends," Woods said, "and wherever he goes I will support him. He's the man who gave me my first shot in a PGA Tour event, the L.A. Open, when I was sixteen. I owe a lot to him. He's been a friend of the family. We visit each other. It's always a pleasure to see him."

It was only logical that he extend an invitation to a prodigy, McLaughlin said. "I viewed it as giving Picasso a paintbrush when he was twelve years old." Still, the promoter's instincts surely helped sway his decision to invite a young amateur who would help boost attendance only marginally in the short term. "I was extremely fortunate to have met him when I did," he said.

Stronger fields mean greater attendance, increasing revenues and expanding the exposure a tournament sponsor receives. McLaughlin's benevolence years earlier created a permanent bond with golf's preeminent headliner, ensuring that Woods is a perpetual entrant in his field, guaranteeing maximum exposure and enormous crowds.

Other tournament directors are without a similar built-in advantage. Their attempts at strengthening their fields have been likened to a college football coach attempting to assemble a formidable roster one recruit at a time, though McLaughlin downplays the notion. "The term *recruiting* is somewhat of a misnomer," he said, citing a variety of factors that influence a player's decision.

"First is where your tournament falls on the schedule, his and yours. Second is the golf course. Three is a lot of other factors."

A player's decision to schedule a particular event is often based on the level of pampering he can expect. This is not a modern development; the late Ky Laffoon was said to have declined to play in the Western Open for no other reason than the unseemly distance between the players' parking lot and the clubhouse.

Woods will play the Western Open from a sense of obligation to McLaughlin. On the other hand, he might never participate in the Bob Hope Chrysler Classic. Once the curator of talent for his own tournament, Hope in his later years has been largely removed from the recruiting process. Yet, after Woods turned pro in 1996, Hope was personally involved in extending Woods an invitation to play in his tournament in January '97. Woods declined and subsequently was skewered publicly by the tournament director, Mike Milthorpe, for having the audacity to stiff an American icon.

"We wrote to Tiger three times, called his father twice, called IMG twice, and never got a return call," Milthorpe said at the time. "I don't mind him not playing. He can go play in Thailand for the rest of his life. I just think if Bob Hope calls you up and asks you to play in his tournament you say, 'Yes.' Mr. Hope is ninety-three years old, and he has done an awful lot for the game of golf. He won't be around forever."

Woods already had agreed to play in the Asian Honda Classic in Bangkok, Thailand, his mother Kultida's hometown, though more than an appeal to pay homage to his heritage was required to secure his commitment. He received a $300,000 appearance fee to play there.

Hope, incidentally, was not the only icon Woods rejected that year. In a letter, South African president Nelson Mandela attempted to persuade Woods to play in the South African Open. He politely declined, citing a scheduling conflict. So it goes with scheduling. Woods, meanwhile, would never pass on the

WGC–American Express Championship, not simply because it offers $1 million to the winner. He is a paid corporate spokesman for American Express. Money speaks more forcefully than an anti-apartheid champion or an aging national treasure.

It spoke volumes when Buick signed Woods to an endorsement contract that pays him upwards of $4 million annually. This ensures that Woods will play in virtually all the Buick Invitationals, Buick Classics, Buick Opens, and Buick Challenges over the next five years. Ben Crenshaw and Steve Elkington are among a handful of other players who have endorsement contracts with Buick and are certain to play in the same events. This, incidentally, need not preclude them from playing in the Mercedes Championship, the Honda Classic, or the Nissan Open on a tour ostensibly bent more on selling cars than golf.

Occasionally, money must whisper, lest it be overheard by the wrong party. Appearance fees are an accepted practice abroad. Woods reportedly received $1 million to play in the Deutsche Bank–SAP Open in Germany in 1999, and he rewarded the sponsor's largesse by winning the tournament. Appearance fees are strictly forbidden on the PGA Tour. In the PGA *Tour Player Handbook and Tournament Regulations*, section VI-A states,

> Neither players nor other individuals acting on such players' behalf shall solicit or accept any compensation, gratuity or other thing of value offered for the purpose of guaranteeing their appearance in any PGA Tour cosponsored, approved or coordinated tournament, including any pro-am played in connection therewith, except as may be specifically authorized by the PGA Tour Policy Board prior to the tournament.

The rule effectively shuts down one recruiting channel on the PGA Tour, though savvy tournament directors and sponsors frequently have navigated their way around this bothersome little obstacle. The cynical might view Woods's endorsement deal with Buick as a cleverly disguised way around the ban on paying appearance fees. Woods's golf bag features the automaker's logo, and that obviously carries a large measure of cachet. But so does his appearance in the tournaments it sponsors.

Years ago, the Honda Classic used to coordinate a pro-am on Monday of tournament week at Lago Mar, a few miles from the tournament site at Weston Hills in Ft. Lauderdale, Florida. A foursome of marquee names played for a substantial appearance fee. The players, a source said, were actually contractually obligated to play in the Honda Classic later in the week. "If those documents had ever become public," the source said, "the shit would have hit the fan."

The grip-and-grin cocktail party or dinner has been another vehicle for securing a player's commitment. In the '80s, a former tournament director said, the Greater Milwaukee Open lured Greg Norman into its fold by paying him $25,000—when that sum was considered substantial in pro golf—to attend a cocktail party and schmooze with sponsors early in the week.

Norman, incidentally, is not likely to play in the Honda Classic again soon, despite the fact that he lives in Hobe Sound, Florida, a short helicopter commute to Coral Springs, where the tournament now is played. Norman once was involved in the production of a made-for-television event in which he played against the best ball of Larry Bird, Ivan Lendl, and Wayne Gretzky. Honda purchased considerable television air time in support of the event, which was played the same year Norman chose to play in the Honda Classic at the TPC at Eagle Trace in Coral Springs. Strong winds added *diabolical* to the growing list of pejoratives used to describe Eagle Trace. "You won't see me here next year," Norman said, disregarding Honda's benevolence toward him. "I don't need to be playing carnival golf." Honda officials were said to have been incensed. The tournament returned to Eagle Trace once, in 1996, from necessity, since its new home, the TPC at Heron Bay, was not yet completed. Norman played, his prior threat notwithstanding. "Sometimes you say things that you shouldn't say and don't really mean," he said. "In my younger days I might have been a little brash. Obviously I don't hold a grudge." The problem with the TPC at Heron Bay is that it was designed by Mark McCumber, whom Norman once accused of cheating, creating an enduring rift. Norman nonetheless has claimed that that will have no bearing on whether he plays there.

The Monday outing or Tuesday cocktail party designed to introduce stars to stargazing sponsors has long been a staple of professional golf and apparently an adequate cover for players receiving appearance fees in violation of the tour rule. The rule—which applies only to the American PGA Tour—is in place to prevent the game from deteriorating into professional tennis, a sport in which paying appearance fees is an accepted practice. Tennis stars with guaranteed money have been known to tank matches early in a tournament, and then beat a hasty retreat to the airport, check in tow for a job not very well done. Golfers similarly have raised suspicions. John Daly once received $100,000 for appearing in the Dutch Open, then shot an 89 in the first round, though he insisted he was trying on every shot. Skewered by the local media, Daly had the event promoter timidly come to his defense. "He's a pretty nice fellow," Robbie van Erwen Dorens said, "but completely crazy."

Another strike against paying appearance fees is that on tours for which it is an accepted practice, players with the drawing power of Woods or Norman often receive sums well in excess of first-place money. Norman received $200,000 to play in the Ford Open in Adelaide, Australia, in 1996. He won the tournament and received first-prize money of $40,500.

Money is not the only incentive that will lure a player from home. A former director of the Greater Milwaukee Open tournament usually faced an uphill battle in attempting to strengthen his field. The tournament often fell later in the year, on a public course outside Milwaukee. The director would approach four of the better hotels in the Milwaukee area and persuade each to donate four suites for the week, which he then would use to entice better players.

Athletes still appreciate (read expect) a handout. A few years ago, John Daly was lured to the Greater Milwaukee Open with the promise of a complimentary suite for the week. When he began pondering his decision to play in a town renowned for breweries, it began to unnerve him. He was a man struggling a day at a time to conquer his alcoholism. Daly feared that the fumes from the breweries might tempt him to sample the local product. It was of sufficient concern that Callaway Golf, his benefactor at the time, dispatched an executive to Milwaukee, in essence to baby-sit for Daly. In 1997, Daly wisely chose not to play in the Las Vegas Invitational. Among his addictions is gambling, and he understood that by going to Vegas he would be placing himself in harm's way. Ruefully, common sense seldom prevails with Daly, who in 1998 chose to ignore his previous concerns and decided to play in Las Vegas, even venturing into a casino one night.

"I had one little slip," Daly said, "but I didn't gamble or drink. I walked into a casino and got scared."

Daly had run into a pair of friends who work for Callaway Golf and offered to bankroll them while he watched. They declined.

"I didn't like the feeling I had being there," Daly said. "It's tough. I like all the fun. Casinos are so much fun. I got scared and left. It was a good test. I know I can't watch."

Daly was miffed that Vegas hotels declined to provide him with a complimentary room. "All the money I've blown in their casinos and they wouldn't even give me a room because I'm not gambling anymore," he said. "The hell with them. I think it's very rude."

Less than a year later, Daly admitted that he was again gambling and drinking, and he returned to the Las Vegas Invitational. After Saturday's round, he was seen leaving the clubhouse with an open bottle of beer in one hand and three or four unopened bottles in his other hand.

Of the factors that dictate a player's schedule, money typically is among the overriding ones. Wayne Levi seemingly would rather play the market than the Masters. A student of finance, Levi has been said to have set his schedule according to the tournaments offering the most prize money. A *Sports Illustrated* story on him noted that he is not averse to playing in late-season events when the quality of the fields is diminished, enhancing his opportunity to cash in.

David Duval, meanwhile, chose to play in the Compaq Classic in New Orleans in 1999 "because the tournament director, Rick George, asked me to play. Nice to be wanted." George routinely travels to tournament sites to acquaint himself with players who might similarly oblige him with their presence in New Orleans. "I went to thirteen events so players could get to know us better," George said. "I remember asking David the first time at the Tour Championship." That was six months earlier.

Mike Nicolette, an obscure part-time tour player, isn't likely ever to miss the B.C. Open. One year there, it began raining as he was en route to the first tee. He sent his caddy on ahead, then dashed across the street to his hotel to collect his rain gear. On his return, a policeman stopped him and denied him access to the course, refusing to believe that he was a player. A shoving match ensued. "Being Italian," Nicolette said, "I had no choice. I punched him. And being that I was half his size, it was no contest. I was down on the ground, two cops were beating on me, and they put on handcuffs. I heard somebody yell that I was a golfer, and then I heard the cop say, 'Not anymore.'" By way of apology, the B.C. Open offered Nicolette an exemption in perpetuity from having to qualify for its tournament.

Family considerations also enter into the equation used to determine schedules. Brandel Chamblee invoked a shopworn reason behind his decision to play the Bay Hill Invitational one year. "I wasn't going to come here," he said, "but my wife was putting me to work for two weeks. That's why I showed up here. I had planned on taking this week off." The National Car Rental Classic at Walt Disney World is a popular tour stop for players with families, for obvious reasons.

The golf course is also a lure, as it has been at the Nissan Open (formerly the Los Angeles Open), a tournament with a long and colorful history that has lost much of its appeal over time. The Riviera Country Club in Pacific Palisades, California, is among the better courses on the PGA Tour, a historic layout on which the U.S. Open was won by Ben Hogan in 1948. Yet it presents a logistical nightmare. Access to the course is via Sunset Boulevard, a crowded, winding four-lane road with numerous traffic lights and few left-turn lanes, and parking is always sparse.

"I don't think any of us like that drive down Sunset Boulevard, then getting to Riviera and not having a place to park," John Daly said, casting his vote for a permanent move to Valencia Country Club, where the Nissan Open was played in 1998 to accommodate the U.S. Senior Open being played at Riviera that year.

Inconvenience can be a death knell.

Woods's schedule, meanwhile, is reasonably predictable. He will play the four major championships—the Masters, U.S. Open, British Open, and PGA Championship—as well as the Players Championship; the Tour Championship; the Western Open; three or four of the Buick events; probably the Nissan Open for its proximity to his hometown of Cypress, California; the WGC–American Express Championship to satisfy an endorsement contract; the Bay Hill Invitational in Orlando, tantamount to a home game for Woods and an event hosted by Arnold Palmer; and the Memorial, hosted by Jack Nicklaus. He also will play the Mercedes Championship, because of its select field (only those who have won on the PGA Tour in the previous year are invited), the WGC–Match Play Championship and the WGC–Invitational in Akron, Ohio, both of which carry a $1 million prize for the winner (Woods won the latter in 1999). Beyond that, he occasionally will play the Las Vegas Invitational, for two reasons: His teacher, Butch Harmon, is headquartered there, and Woods is an enthusiastic participant of games of chance. The National Car Rental Golf Classic at Walt Disney World is also in his neighborhood, and he will probably participate in that as well.

His international schedule is dictated largely by the sums of guaranteed money he can generate. Aside from playing the British Open, Woods is not likely to venture abroad without incentive in the form of a substantial stipend.

Obviously every PGA Tour event wants him in its field, though several of them aren't likely ever to be so fortunate. Tournament directors once proposed a three-and-one rule, requiring each player to participate in every PGA Tour event at least once in a three-year period. The Tour hierarchy vigorously and successfully argued against it, aware that its constituents, as independent contractors, would protest.

So it is left to the creativity and depth of pockets of tournament directors to attempt to strengthen their fields by whatever legal (or even questionable) means are at their disposal. The winner ultimately is the player.

"It's a can-you-top-this kind of thing," McLaughlin said. "We try to outdo each other on amenities, trying to get a little angle."

McLaughlin and the Western Open play the angle to perfection, though the two hundred Motorola cell phones it issued one year for contestants' use during the week might have been a mistake. One month later, eighty phones were still outstanding.

On Tuesday night of tournament week, they host a show for the players and their families at the Drury Lane Theatre in nearby Oak Brook. One year, they sought Grammy winner Whitney Houston, offering her $250,000 to perform for an hour. She declined, citing the fact that she does not do private gigs. The tournament raised the ante to $350,000 for an hour's work. She declined again, and the risk factor was revealed. When she does a public concert, her audience is made up of fans paying for the privilege of hearing her, ensuring a warm, heartfelt, enthusiastic response that is not guaranteed at a private function. The tournament went to Plan B, Jerry Seinfeld, at the height of the popularity of his television sitcom, and he agreed to do a one-hour stand-up comedy routine for $250,000.

The Western Open brought Kenny G to perform one year, Bill Cosby another. The Cirque du Soleil was hired for a night to entertain the players and their families. McLaughlin once arranged to rent Comiskey Park in Chicago, so that players could take their kids onto the field to frolic. The tournament routinely secures White Sox or Cubs tickets for players.

It also hosts a barbecue and fireworks show for the players and their families on the Thursday night of the event at a park not far from the golf course. This is an especially popular perk inasmuch as no outsiders are welcome, so there is no press to avoid and no sponsors to glad-hand. Nick Price once injured his shoulder, causing him to withdraw on the eve of the tournament. Nonetheless, he and his family remained in the Chicago area so they could attend the barbecue and fireworks show.

The Western always has had an exceptional child-care program, the Wee Western, ferrying players' kids to various locales, including the American Science and History Museum, while their fathers worked.

Every angle is explored and exploited by tournament directors:

• The Shell Houston Open asked Houston Rockets star Charles Barkley to intervene on its behalf in its attempt to get Woods into the field. Barkley offered Woods his home and his limousine for the week.

• The Greater Vancouver Open appealed to players' wives to help strengthen the field for its inaugural tournament, scheduled opposite the NEC–World Series of Golf in 1996. It invited them to make a vacation of it and, among other activities, scheduled trips to nearby Victoria Island for tea at the renowned Empress Hotel.

• Australia's Greg Norman played in the Spanish Open in 1997 at the request of Spain's Seve Ballesteros, who agreed to reciprocate by playing in the Holden Classic in Australia the following year.

The Sprint International is said to be among the PGA Tour leaders in pampering players, and it begins the moment they arrive at the airport. When Scott McCarron was a rookie, he played the Sprint International at Castle Pines and was indelibly impressed by how he was treated when he arrived there, particularly by a clubhouse attendant, Tom Horal. "He treated me as if I were Jack Nicklaus," McCarron said.

As one disgruntled tournament director weary of the rising cost of competing put it, the tournament director at the Sprint "is offering dry-cleaning, for God's sake. Players might as well just bring all their dirty laundry." And the list goes on.

The bone-weary might want to play in the Compaq Classic in New Orleans, which has a masseuse on call for players in need of a rubdown. It also offers players the opportunity to fish for redfish early in the week, transporting them afterward by helicopter to the practice tee.

The MCI Classic in Hilton Head, South Carolina, offers on-site condominiums, gratis for past champions. This ranks among the better perks available on a tour with no shortage of them. One former champion, Davis Love III, brought his fishing boat, the *LexSea*, one year, choosing to stay on it rather than using the condominium offered him. The tournament picked up his moorage fee. The tournament also transforms a house owned by the Heritage Classic Foundation near the tenth tee into a hospitality house offering twenty-four-hour food service for players. In 1999, Tiger Woods hit his tee shot at the tenth hole, ran to the house, and emerged with a couple of hot dogs to fuel him on his back-nine trek.

Another useful courtesy extended personally by Steve Wilmot, director of the MCI Classic tournament, is that he closely monitors the PGA Tour's official commit list. He mails reminders to those players who have unofficially committed to the tournament by informing him they were coming, yet who haven't officially entered by phoning the tour office. This would seem to be an unnecessary courtesy, yet at least once a year a player shows up at a tournament in which he failed to enter:

- Ireland's David Feherty, the tour pro turned irreverent CBS broadcaster, was new to the PGA Tour and had failed to grasp its procedures. He wanted to play in the Freeport–McMoran Classic one year but misfiled his commitment forms. "I called to ask them to pick me up from the airport, and they said, 'Why? Are you coming to be a marshal or something?'" Feherty said.

- Mark O'Meara arrived at the Riviera Country Club to play in the Nissan Open in 1995, only to discover that he had failed to enter. To fill the gap it created in his schedule, he entered the Honda Classic two weeks later and won the event.

- Davis Love III was at home in Sea Island, Georgia, preparing to travel to Los Angeles for the Nissan Open in 1998, when the phone rang. It was a friend who had noticed that Love's name was missing from the tournament's entry list. Love then phoned the *Los Angeles Times* for an updated list. Love's name was not on it. The following morning, Love phoned the PGA Tour office and discovered that he had failed to enter. "I was more than packed," Love said. "I was literally going to bed. I had an eight o'clock flight out. I've had back luck in Los Angeles. Two no-commits, a kidney stone, and I got beat in a playoff."

Wilmot's diligence ensures that no such lapse occurs at his event, which in itself qualifies as a perk. If only his diligence extended to passports and visas:

- Fred Couples was en route to the British Open one year and was changing planes in Chicago when he realized that he had left his passport home in Palm Springs, California. He had to fly home to retrieve it, transforming a long trip to Great Britain into an extraordinarily long trip. Couples also drove from his home in Santa Barbara, California, to La Quinta, California, for the Diners Club Matches, only to learn that the Diners Club Matches had moved to Newport Coast, California, two hours away.
- Greg Norman once flew to Spain without a visa, and Spanish officials escorted him to the next plane to London.

In 1996, the Anheuser-Busch Classic had the misfortune of being played the week before the British Open at Royal Lytham. To shore up its field, it chartered two planes to ferry players from Kingsmill, Virginia, to the Newark, New Jersey, airport for the flight abroad. It also provided free passes to Busch Gardens; day care for players' kids, which included trips to Colonial Williamsburg, Busch Gardens, and other area sites; and a Tuesday night barbecue with a band, pony rides, clowns, and a fireworks show.

Only one charter airplane was necessary, and it could have been a diminutive one. Only three players—Curtis Strange, Jay Haas, and Mark McCumber—took advantage of the free transport to Newark. The tournament attracted only one of the top fifty money winners, Hoch, who won the tournament, leading wire to wire.

• • •

Tournament week begins in earnest at the departure gate. On one end of the spectrum is Greg Norman, whose travel toys run the gamut, though he would prefer they not be called toys. For tournaments up the coast from his Hobe Sound, Florida, home (the MCI Classic on Hilton Head Island, South Carolina, for instance), he might travel via his one-hundred-forty-four-foot yacht, the *Aussie Rules*, or, as one MCI Classic official called Norman's ship anchored out on Calibogue Sound, the *Queen Mary*. Though limited mooring is available for ships of that size, none was available in 1999, and Norman had to anchor in mid-harbor and commute to shore on a water shuttle. This yacht, incidentally, was purchased to replace an eighty-six-foot fishing boat, prompting Bob Verdi to write in *Golf World* magazine that it "looks more like a yacht on which, if you absolutely had to have a fish, you probably would call room service."

For inland events that require air travel, Norman's Gulfstream GV is standing by. Norman had ordered a Boeing 737 Business Jet, a $38 million investment that would have enabled him to fly from South Florida to Australia with only one fuel stop required. Given that many small airports cannot accommodate larger jets, Norman reconsidered and canceled the order, choosing instead to upgrade from his GIV to a GV.

For tournaments closer to home, he has a Bell 430 jet helicopter waiting on a pad adjacent to his home, a fortunate acquisition that paid dividends at the Doral-Ryder Open in 1996. Shortly before he teed off in the final round, the face of his Cobra driver caved in as he was hitting balls on the practice tee. He phoned his wife, Laura, who summoned the pilot and used the Bell 430 to ferry a replacement driver to the golf course in time for Norman's round. Later that day, he won the tournament.

This use of an expensive piece of machinery only served to reinforce what he steadfastly insists, that these are not toys. "I derive as much gratification from my other business interests as I do from golf," Norman told *Golf Digest*. "Some of my fellow players looked at me kind of funny when I showed up at a tournament in Florida in a helicopter. But you can waste a lot of hours without it, and I can't be worried about what other people say or think. My plane and my helicopter are the furthest things from being toys you could ever imagine."

Tiger Woods is among the growing legion of players who travel by private corporate jet, though their number diminished by one when Payne Stewart died tragically aboard a Learjet. When Woods turned pro in 1996, he purchased from Warren Buffett's company, Executive Jets, a one-eighth share of a Citation X, the same kind of plane Arnold Palmer flies. In return, Woods has a Citation X at his disposal anytime, anywhere in the world, provided he gives four hours' notice. The cost is exorbitant: $2.1 million for the one-eighth share, management fees of $14,200 a month, and an hourly rate of $1,920.

Those fortunate enough to live in the exclusive Isleworth community in Windermere, Florida, that Woods calls home are occasionally invited to travel on TWA, as players jokingly call it—Tiger Woods Airlines. "I don't get any frequent flier miles," Woods's neighbor and friend Mark O'Meara said, "but the service is pretty good."

Davis Love III, Ben Crenshaw, and Paul Azinger are among others traveling by private jet. It affords them the opportunity to take off immediately following play on Sunday, enabling them to spend more time at home—as many as twenty-five extra days a year, by Love's count. The tour also has a growing squadron of pilots who either own or lease jets or planes and provide their own transportation to tournament sites. Among them are Phil Mickelson and Bill Glasson.

Meanwhile, Brandel Chamblee told how he decided to charter a jet at $4,500 for his first trip to the Masters. When he informed his wife that he had done so, she was astounded. "Honey,"

Chamblee said, attempting to explain the lavish expenditure, "you can't take a pocketknife into a gunfight."

At the other end of this spectrum are those players concerned more with paying bills than winning tournaments. They fly coach, stay in budget motels, even travel by car or van when possible. "When Sunday rolls around and you all run out to Butler Aviation," David Ogrin said in a *Golf Digest* interview, "and hop onto your GIIs or GIVs or whatever, there tends to be a different clique from the guys running down to Southwest Airlines, and a lot different from the guys piling into a Chevy and heading off to the next event."

In between the haves and the have-nots is the inimitable John Daly, who at one time could have easily afforded first-class air travel, yet preferred modes of transport that can't fall out of the sky. A fear of flying (as well as the fact that airlines do not permit smoking) moved Daly to purchase a motor home in which he often traveled. Daly, of course, does nothing in a small, modest way. This is evident again in the motor home he dubbed "The Ride." It cost him $780,000 and was equipped with a washer and dryer, satellite television, surround-sound stereo, full kitchen, and bedroom. He traveled the country in it, staying in campsites rather than hotels. Daly once parked the motor home in a seedy RV park near Hilton Head. His friend Fuzzy Zoeller stopped by for a visit, cast a wary eye at the ramshackle surroundings, and said later, "That's as close as I ever want to get to poverty."

Daly began selling off his luxury automobiles to pay mounting gambling bills. Toward the end of the 1999 season, he was seen traveling in a Chevrolet van, with his trademark swing motto, "Grip it and rip it," emblazoned on each side and a vanity license plate that read, "PGA '91," recalling a victory that thrust him to the pinnacle of golf, from which he has followed a long, tortuous path downhill.

Then there is Frank Lickliter, who occasionally travels from his home in Ponte Vedra Beach, Florida, using his Humvee. When he revealed that he planned to drive it to Augusta, Georgia, for the Masters, he no doubt caused a few brows to furrow among the green-jacket brigade there. "Someone wrote I was going to knock over some trees," Lickliter said, "which I'm sure the gentlemen at Augusta appreciated."

Once players arrive at a tournament site, new courtesy cars typically await them—an extraordinary cost to all involved, including the car manufacturers, who are required to absorb $3,000 or more per car in depreciation. "It's something the auto manufacturers are looking at very, very strongly," McLaughlin said.

This would not be welcome news on the PGA Tour, where the definition of a crisis is *not* a three-putt or a double bogey, but the loss of the courtesy car. It nearly happened at the Buick Open in Grand Blanc, Michigan, in 1998, when strikes at two General Motors plants in Flint, Michigan, left tournament organizers scrambling to come up with the one hundred eighty cars required for the week.

Courtesy cars typically are available to every player in the field. Players have the use of the car for the entire week, gratis, and are instructed as to where to return it, though they don't always pay attention. The Bob Hope Chrysler Classic gives courtesy cars to the top hundred players in the field, provided they haven't abused the privilege in previous years and been removed from the list. The players are to return their cars to the Palm Springs Airport. Often players show up at Ontario Airport, at least an hour away, and occasionally they have left cars in the short-term parking lot there. Two cars once were reported missing and eventually turned up at the tiny Thermal Airport in the middle of the desert south of the Palm Springs area. Thermal may not be the last place on earth one would attempt to find a lost car, but it is in contention. Other cars have been dropped off in Phoenix, a state away.

A Western Open courtesy car once turned up in Rockford, Illinois, eighty-three miles northwest of Chicago. Another was lost for three months before the general manager of a local hotel phoned tournament headquarters to report that a courtesy car had been gathering dust in the hotel parking lot. McLaughlin said he has had a new courtesy car returned with five thousand miles on it.

The United States Golf Association decided to offer courtesy cars to U.S. Open participants for the first time at Shinnecock Hills on Long Island in 1986. The USGA conducted a pool on the furthest point a courtesy car would turn up. The winner: White Plains Airport in Westchester County, New York.

John Daly was playing in the Franklin Templeton Shark Shootout in 1996 and used the Chevy Tahoe courtesy SUV each player had at his disposal to drive to Las Vegas and back three times that week, a ten-hour round trip. "I think mine needed an oil change," he said.

Occasionally, cars come back banged up. At the Bay Hill Invitational in 1997, Jeff Maggert was involved in a minor traffic accident. "I just hope I don't get banned from the courtesy car list next year," Maggert said, presumably in jest. Robert Gamez had to withdraw from the Kemper Open when he suffered a bruised spleen and liver after his courtesy car slid off a wet road and crashed into a tree two days before the tournament began.

The fastidious Mark O'Meara is the only player known to have washed his courtesy car. Doug Tewell once asked to exchange his car for one that came equipped with a cassette deck. "They thought I was crazy," he said. Tewell in fact uses various songs as focal points during tournaments. Thus a cassette deck was required to enable him to listen to the requisite songs.

The first time Tiger Woods drove a Mercedes Benz was two months after turning pro in 1996. The Tour Championship provided each of the thirty players in the field with a Mercedes courtesy car to drive for the week. Woods immediately was smitten, even though the car was out of its element in the places where he most wanted to drive it at that point in his life—the drive-through windows at McDonald's and Taco Bell.

"Why don't you get one?" his teacher Butch Harmon said to Tiger, who had not yet shed his naïveté and hadn't considered that with his $60 million in contracts he could afford a fleet of them.

"You know how much one of these costs?" he replied, startled that anyone might suggest he spend that much.

A few months later, Woods was given one for winning the Mercedes Championship. He presented the keys to his mother, Kultida. By then, Woods better comprehended the size of his fortune.

Among other perks that are standard fare on the PGA Tour is free phone use in the clubhouse, as well as free lunch for players and their families. Tournament directors once complained to the former PGA Tour commissioner Deane Beman that players were abusing their privileges, sometimes by bringing a dozen friends and family members into the players' dining room for lunch, the cost—fifteen dollars or more a head—being absorbed by the tour-nament.

"Deane said to get rid of the courtesy cars, the phones, the lunch, and the players will still come," McLaughlin said, though he knows better. Membership, too many players have come to expect, has its privileges. One young player once discovered he was not on the list to receive a courtesy car, and he began to berate a volunteer working on the transportation committee. Peter Jacobsen overheard him and enlisted the help of Greg Norman to deliver a stern lecture to the young man, informing him in pointed language that the game owes him nothing, least of all a free ride.

"The younger players are really assholes," one tournament director said. "There are some younger players and their wives who may not appreciate everything done for them."

Arnold Palmer concurs. "I don't think modern tour players

know the difference," he said in *Golf* magazine. "They don't know it isn't supposed to be this way."

Occasionally the tournament gets it wrong, however. Lanny Wadkins, a PGA Championship winner, Ryder Cup captain, and two-time winner of the Los Angeles Open, once inexplicably was not on the courtesy car list at the Nissan (formerly Los Angeles) Open. Jeff Sluman witnessed the slight and made a plea with the transportation director on Wadkins's behalf, even offering to surrender his own courtesy car.

This would represent the ultimate, though not the only, sacrifice made in this red-carpet world. There also is the proverbial sacrificial lamb, herbed and roasted and augmented perhaps with raspberry *beurre blanc* sauce, a gourmet feast in any other setting. On the PGA Tour, where it stands in tribute to a lifestyle to which most only aspire, it represents lunch.

Or, as John Daly once said, "The cuisine ... You're talking about food, right?"

2

WANDS OF WAR

The most spirited rivalries in golf take place not inside the ropes but behind the scenes, on the practice tee on Tuesday of tournament week. The players have recognizable names—Callaway, Titleist, Taylor Made, Ping, Wilson, and Cobra, among others—and they are vying for the most cherished prize in golf from their perspective: the consumer.

Equipment manufacturers keep supplies of their products in a roped-off corral adjacent to the practice tee at tournament sites. Their tour reps assiduously work the tee line on Tuesdays, tending the needs of players under contract and extolling the virtues of their equipment lines to those who have yet to see the light. The reps' job is to get their product into as many bags as possible, to fortify their companies' "tour presence," in order to sell more of their products to the public golfer. The equipment, of course, is free to the player.

"If you need a new club you just walk up to someone and say, 'Hey, I need a club,'" the Australian pro Bradley Hughes said.

When John Daly and Callaway Golf parted company, Daly became a free agent, entitled to use any equipment he wished. The next time he turned up in a PGA Tour event, he had replaced his Callaway Great Big Bertha Hawk Eye titanium driver with a Titleist 975D titanium driver. A week later, he had replaced his Callaway X-12 irons with Titleist DCI 990 irons. Of his fourteen clubs, in fact, thirteen were manufactured by Titleist.

This was the result of Steve Mata's diligence. Mata is Titleist's tour rep and among the best at working the practice tee, servicing existing accounts and attempting to create new ones. Mata began his career at Taylor Made, but he was enticed by a significant pay increase to join Titleist in the fall of 1997. Titleist was introducing a new titanium driver that it wished to circulate on the PGA Tour, and Mata was hired to tap into his close associations with a vast number of tour players, who over the years had grown to like and respect him.

Among Mata's friendships was one with Daly, though the two had never represented the same company. Once Daly and Callaway had severed ties and the former no longer was contractually obligated to play with Callaway clubs, Mata suggested that Daly give the Titleist 975D a test drive. Daly agreed, and the club was in his bag immediately. Of course, he would agree to try the new Titleist DCI 990 irons as well.

Advantage Mata and Titleist.

This is a scenario that unfolds weekly on the PGA Tour. Since equipment manufacturers are acutely aware of the public's voracious appetite to use what the pros use, they dispense free equipment as though it were advice. In the days leading to a typical mid-season event, Callaway Golf, for instance, hands out between twenty and forty drivers and a like number of fairway woods.

Of course, what the pros use often only superficially resembles what the public purchases from the rack and often bears no resemblance whatsoever to it. Tiger Woods, for instance, has been playing with Titleist prototype irons for more than three years. The irons were built for him after he turned pro in 1996 and signed an equipment contract with Titleist. These particular irons are not available to the public. Jack Nicklaus requires that his clubs be built to precise specifications that take the concept "custom-built" to levels inaccessible to the buying public.

Tour players often have a series of minor surgeries performed on their clubs to alter their playing characteristics, in effect customizing them to their particular swings. Lead tape, typically applied behind the club face, is a staple of professional golfers' irons. Justin Leonard has the heels of his irons ground, enabling him to work the ball better. To replace the weight removed by grounding, he uses pieces of lead tape. Leonard also had two holes drilled in the back of his 56-degree wedge to remove weight. Davis Love III uses lead tape on all his Titleist irons to ensure that they're uniform, all D-4 swing weights.

Mark O'Meara is among a handful of players who have grown attached to their wedges and choose not to discard them even as the grooves wear out. O'Meara has had the faces of his wedges ground out and replaced with Carbite faces.

Equipment companies transform trailers into mobile workshops that are driven tournament to tournament and set up near the practice tee to accommodate players with equipment concerns. Some players, notably Jesper Parnevik, frequent the trailers, changing shafts and grips so often that what they end up using is akin to a new set of clubs each time. Parnevik alters his equipment so often that a Callaway employee dubbed the process "Jesperizing."

Parnevik put a new set of Callaway irons into play at the Greater Greensboro Chrysler Classic in 1999 and won the tournament. When he was asked why he was using new irons, he demonstrated how he became the king of club tinkering. "I fooled around a little bit at Augusta," he said. "I had one new set at Augusta because I wanted to try to get the ball flight higher. But they didn't feel the way I wanted. I changed last week to a low kick-point shaft to shoot the ball up a little bit more. I've seen Greg Norman, and he hits it pretty high. But it just didn't feel right, so I got some new heads and went back to my old shafts and did some grinding and now it feels great again."

Parnevik is perpetually attempting to find the combination of club specifications best suited to create particular shots. "There are some guys who want a 7-iron that they can hit one-hundred-sixty-five yards," an equipment rep explained. "Jesper might want a

7-iron he can hit from one hundred fifty to one hundred ninety yards."

The combinations are endless. A dozen or more shaft companies offer their wares on tour, and each company has a variety of shaft offerings, with different kick points or different torques or shaft flexes. "Enter that into the equation, especially for guys who like to tinker, and we'll have orders of five to ten drivers from a single player," one rep said.

Parnevik's putters do not have a particularly long shelf life, either. He falls in and out of love with them at a frenetic pace. "It's hard to accept it's your fault when you've missed a putt," he said. "So you're looking for that magic one that might turn your career around and work every time. I haven't found one yet. I don't know what happens. You pick one out because you like it, but it seems like [the magic] disappears after a while and I don't know where it goes."

Fulton Allem, the South African who won the NEC World Series of Golf in 1993, is notorious for tinkering with his clubs. He won the World Series using a different Callaway driver in each of the four rounds at Firestone Country Club. At the U.S. Open two years later, Allem changed the shafts in his irons four times on Monday, without so much as playing a single hole with any of them. Eventually, he wound up with his original shafts.

Larry Nelson won the U.S. Open at Oakmont in 1983 playing with three different sets of irons, a remarkable achievement given the precision required to win at the professional level.

Others, like Tom Lehman, a Taylor Made staff player, seldom alter their clubs once they've tweaked them to their satisfaction. "I'm probably the least nuisance to Taylor Made of any guy out on tour," Lehman told *Golf Digest*. "You'll see me in their tour van about once every six months. That's how I like it, and how they like it, too."

R. W. Eaks tweaks his equipment to such an extent that he acknowledges he is "kind of psycho about that stuff." He said he prefers that his irons be one degree flat, yet he once wound up with a set that was five degrees upright. Eventually, he had the clubs bent until they were two or three degrees upright, at which point he was satisfied, though only momentarily.

Paul Azinger used to say that he was certain to defeat anyone still tinkering with his equipment on Wednesday. There are exceptions, Arnold Palmer among them. Palmer habitually tinkers with his equipment and has done so for his entire career. He once asked Mata if he'd mind decreasing the loft of a 1-iron for him. Mata took the club to one of the equipment trailers and performed the requested surgery. He returned the club to Palmer, who began lashing long, straight shots with it.

"What do you think?" Mata asked.

"If it came any better than that," Palmer said, "God would have kept it for himself."

Palmer is a godsend to the tour rep. He is a marquee star willing to experiment with anyone's club. Should he cotton to a club's performance on the practice tee, it will earn a place in his tournament arsenal, even at the expense of a club manufactured by his own equipment company. That happened at the Masters this year, when he had an Orlimar TriMetal fairway wood in his bag, hidden beneath a Palmer Golf Company head cover—immaculate deception by the King.

There is always a concern that a player might grow attached to a club other than one he is being paid to use. Among Mata's tasks is to keep at bay competitors attempting to get their clubs into the hands of Tiger Woods, who is paid $2 million annually to play with Titleist woods and irons.

Given his overwhelming success, why would Tiger change anything? The answer is that the golfer's quest to improve is insatiable, even at Woods's level. In his first year as a professional, he began hitting drives with a Cobra prototype driver, which featured a gripless shaft. He was bombing the ball with it and wondered aloud to his teacher Butch Harmon whether he could put the club into his bag. Harmon gently reminded him that additional length was not a priority, that controlling the length he already had was more important.

Even players under contract are easily persuaded to experiment. Paul Stankowski, a member of the Callaway stable, once attempted to shake a slump by replacing his Callaway irons with his old Ping irons, much to the chagrin of the company for which he was working. This was a faux pas compounded by poor timing; Callaway was in the midst of a crusade against competitors who trumpeted their brands on, say, the side of a golf bag that contained none of that brand's products. In a timely fax, Callaway sternly admonished Stankowski, who returned the Callaway irons to his bag the next day.

"I've studied this game for twenty-seven years," Gary Player said, speaking of the players' eternal quest to find a magic wand, "and I know an awful lot about nothing. Golf is like a puzzle without an answer. It's something indescribable. That's the fascination of the game. You get a new driver or putter, and you feel there's something in that driver or putter, and all of a sudden everything clicks."

Sometimes the clubs need not click to find their way into bags. Companies typically offer financial incentives for players to use their equipment. When one company presented its new driver, it was offering a package deal: $1,500 a week for anyone using the driver as well as one of its putters. When Titleist began winning the driver count, Callaway was said to have responded by increasing its weekly stipend to those using one of its drivers. Companies usually offer token remuneration for players using their driver or putter, with bonuses awarded to those who win with their equipment.

Even the obscure journeyman or untested rookie without a club contract receives his equipment free and can at least defray expenses by judiciously choosing his equipment, or, closer to the truth, selling out to the highest bidder.

Some players accept the reps' various offerings, though they have no intention of using the product. These are the men known in the industry as club collectors. What they do with their stockpile is anyone's guess, though the consensus is that their family and friends ultimately are the benefactors. One Senior PGA Tour player once showed up at the PGA Seniors' Championship even though he was not in the field, and was spotted leaving with about six dozen balls and a few new clubs.

One manufacturer's rep divided the players into four categories. One is the player who returns all equipment he cannot hit with or won't use. Two is the player who tells the rep that he does not want the club, but he knows someone who does. Three is the player who accepts the club with no intention of ever using it. Four is the player who requests several clubs, with or without the intention of using them.

The manner in which players view their equipment varies from idiosyncratic to apathetic. Fred Couples was born gifted, with the ability to hit quality shots with anything put into his hands, even presumably a broomstick. "He might be the best feel player in the history of the game," said Dave Boone, who built Couples's clubs for him at Lynx, the company with which he had an endorsement contract for most of the nineties.

Couples might have no idea what the lie and loft of his irons are, yet he recognizes what he wants according to nothing more scientific than how the clubs feel in his hands. In December of 1991, after he had signed a contract to represent Lynx the following year, Couples was playing in the Johnnie Walker World Championship in Jamaica. Boone traveled there to show Couples the new Lynx Parallax irons, similar to those he would be using in 1992 and beyond. Boone had no intention of permitting Couples to use this particular set, since it hadn't been built to his specifications—not that that is critical with Couples.

When Boone took the irons into the clubhouse in Jamaica, Couples had not yet arrived. Davis Love III spotted Boone with the Lynx irons.

"Hey, you got Freddie's new irons there?" Love asked, separating the 5-iron from the rest of the set and testing it with a couple of waggles.

"That looks perfect," Love said.

Steve Elkington took the 7-iron and was similarly impressed. Another iron passed Greg Norman's inspection. Soon Couples's clubs were scattered around the clubhouse. Then Couples walked in.

"Where are my new clubs?" he asked, seeing them spread out among his competitors. Couples gathered them up, took a brief look at them, and announced to his caddy, Joe LaCava, "Joe, we're playing with these today."

"LaCava had this look of absolute terror," Boone said.

Boone was concerned because the irons had not been fitted for Couples. But Couples's ability is such that he is able to compensate for any deviation from a perfect fit. He put the clubs into play and easily won the Johnnie Walker World Championship against a prestigious field.

Couples eventually won the Masters with those irons, though he never was comfortable with the original 8-iron. He called it "a penalty club," though his first career hole in one was made with that 8-iron. However, he loved the 9-iron and asked Boone whether he could take another 9-iron and turn it into an 8-iron.

"There's absolutely no way you can do it," Boone said.

Boone eventually cobbled together an 8-iron by tweaking one that had been made for Ernie Els, another Lynx client at the time. Couples was satisfied.

Grips were another issue with Couples. "We'd put them on and line them up perfectly with a laser," Boone said, "and he'd say, 'They're not right.'" One time, after the grips were attached to

Couples's satisfaction, Boone inspected them. "They were all off," he said. Couples's only barometer was how they felt in his hands.

The summer before he won the Masters, Couples was visiting his friend Tom Watson in Kansas City and was attracted to a Ram 3-wood in the trunk of Watson's car. He was immediately smitten by its looks and feel. He asked Watson if he could have it. Watson, suspecting that the club belonged to his wife, readily gave it up. The club became one of Couples's favorites and was in his bag the following spring when he won at Augusta.

Nick Faldo is the antithesis of Couples; he is meticulous about his equipment, possibly to a fault. He will inform a tour rep that a club is 1/16th of an inch too long or short and will demand that it be corrected. Seve Ballesteros simply eyeballs a club and can tell whether it sets up a degree too flat or a degree too upright.

Mark O'Meara is a meticulous sort. Since he wants his equipment to look new, he sends his clubs to the Taylor Made factory every few months for a buff-and-polish job to restore their luster.

Then there are those who need standby implements. Among them is Mark Calcavecchia, whose drivers frequently meet an untimely demise, victims of too many errant drives in concert with Calcavecchia's tempestuous nature. Calcavecchia once slammed the head of his driver against a cart path, snapping it off and sending it soaring into the gallery, nearly hitting a woman. "She made sure everyone knew I was a jerk," Calcavecchia said, recalling that she informed tournament officials as well as a newspaper reporter. "Obviously, I haven't done that again."

Death by drowning is another time-honored way of dispensing punishment. This recalls the time Craig Stadler arrived at a tournament site with a new putter. Why, he was asked, a new putter?

"The old one," he replied without hesitation, "didn't float."

When Callaway Golf had its endorsement agreement with Daly, entire sets of clubs had to be standing by. When the mood struck him, generally when he was disgusted after an indifferent round, he was known to give away everything—his entire set, bag included—to the first kid he spotted near the eighteenth green. More typically, though, he discarded his driver, which betrayed him more often than its brethren in the golf bag.

He gave his clubs away provided they survived the round intact. At the seventeenth hole at the FedEx St. Jude Classic one year, Daly hooked a 5-iron shot out of bounds. His playing partner, Loren Roberts, said he never saw Daly actually break the club, but when he looked over, the 5-iron was in two pieces.

Daly, in fact, purchased large quantities of Callaway Golf equipment, which he gave away in lieu of discarding his own sets. A Callaway Golf executive had discouraged Daly from giving away his own equipment, noting that the clubs built to his specs were worthless in the hands of a less skilled player incapable of producing the same clubhead speed. "I'm not sure anybody could hit a set of the irons we built for him," the Callaway official said. Or a driver built for him.

Daly tends to draw the ball, which too often overreacts and results in the dreaded out-of-control hook. In an attempt to hit a fade, he sought help from Peter Booth, Callaway Golf's tour rep, who left for a few minutes and returned with a driver with only 6.5 degrees of loft and an industrial-strength shaft. Daly hit towering drives with the club, which would have been useless in another's hands. Another PGA Tour player, Ted Tryba, attempted to use it and produced only a weak, low fade.

Professional golfers, incidentally, are similar to their amateur brethren in that they, too, are curious about what the pros are using. This is how new products turn up in players' bags. When Nick Faldo won the Masters using an Odyssey putter, others on the PGA Tour began to experiment with one. Eventually Odyssey won the putter count on the PGA Tour.

Putters generally have the shortest life span on the PGA Tour.

The putter is a player's money club, so when it ceases to pay its way it can be benched quickly.

The putter with which Payne Stewart won the AT&T Pebble Beach National Pro-Am and the U.S. Open in 1999 was obtained in a familiar fashion; it was given to him by a tour rep offering his wares in the days preceding a tournament. On the day before the AT&T began, a representative of the SeeMore Putter Company approached Stewart's caddy, Mike Hicks, and pitched him on the benefits of a SeeMore putter.

"Payne, you need to check this out," Hicks said to him.

Stewart began working with it and was impressed with the results in practice.

"It took a little getting used to," he said. "If you look at Mark O'Meara, he's probably one of the best putters we have out on tour and his hands are back here and it's just a shoulder movement. That's what this putter does; rather than a forward press that delofts the putter, it makes me keep my hands back and keeps the proper loft on the club. The ball has been rolling wonderfully. It's very exciting."

By Sunday of that week, Stewart was a winner on the PGA Tour for the first time in four years. A few months later, he won his second U.S. Open by holing a dramatic fifteen-foot par putt on the seventy-second hole with that SeeMore putter.

In the heat of the moment in 1991, Jay Don Blake discarded a putter of which he had grown weary. He was playing a money game with friends at the Springs Club in Rancho Mirage, California, when the putter he had used for the better part of twenty years, an Acushnet Bulls Eye, failed him once too often for its own good. At the seventeenth hole, he missed a short putt, a crime for which the sentence was death. He sent the putter on a short trek into a pond.

"I'd been struggling with it for a couple of weeks," he said, "and I was playing with some friends. We kind of had a little money game going. I got tired of missing putts. I couldn't get anything to go in. I got irritated, and I gave the putter a little whirly-bird into the lake. It was very much out of character. I don't know what came over me. I just decided I didn't want the thing anymore."

That was not entirely the case. His father had given him the putter twenty years earlier, and upon reflection Blake decided he wanted it back. He asked an assistant pro at the Springs Club to see whether the putter could be fished out of the pond.

Meanwhile, Blake had a tournament to play, the Shearson Lehman Brothers Open at Torrey Pines in La Jolla, California. Absent the Bulls Eye putter, he put a new Ray Cook Blue Goose in his bag. In the final round, he holed an eighteen-foot downhill putt from off the green for birdie at fifteen and a fifteen-foot putt for birdie at the seventeenth hole, enabling him to win for the first time as a professional.

Billy Ray Brown took an unacceptable thirty-five putts with his putter one day, then handed it to a boy standing by the eighteenth green. "You can have this," Brown said, "but don't try putting with it."

A series of missed cuts and another missed putt moved Woody Austin to take out his frustration on himself at the MCI Classic in 1997. He began banging his putter against his head, five times in all, bending the putter's shaft. "They just don't make putters like they used to," he said.

Dudley Hart was given the nickname "Mini Volcano" to account for his temper, which occasionally went unchecked early in his career. He once was asked whether he ever snapped a club.

"You don't have enough paper for that," he said. "I've done a lot of that, usually post-round stuff. You finish and you don't like the putter and you kind of go in the locker room, step on it and say, 'Put this one to rest, it didn't work very well.'"

Old habits die hard. The son of a club professional, Hart often broke clubs in his formative years, but he learned to reshaft them himself and would do so quickly, lest his father find out. His father knew, however. "My dad told me that he knew I was breaking them and reshafting them," Hart said, "because every shaft was different."

He has worked diligently on curbing his temper, though occasionally it still resurfaces. At the Greater Milwaukee Open in 1996, he hit a tee shot at the eighteenth hole that required justice to be rendered swiftly on his miscreant driver. He slammed it into the turf, and, of course, the shaft broke. "I didn't mean to break it," he said. "The shaft wasn't as durable as I thought it was."

As is his habit, Ken Green once tossed his putter to his caddy, who was not paying attention that particular time and never saw the airborne implement. It sailed past him and into the alligator-infested pond surrounding the island green at the seventeenth hole at the TPC at Sawgrass in Ponte Vedra, Florida. Green was required to putt with his 2-iron on the eighteenth hole. At least no one was hurt. That nearly was not the case once when Green flipped his putter to his caddy and nearly clipped Payne Stewart in the nose. "Missed me by about two inches," Stewart said. "If it had hit me, it would have gone back to him in two pieces."

Paul Azinger missed a short putt at the ninth hole of the British Open one year and reacted angrily, snapping the shaft of his putter in half. "I putt better with my sand wedge anyway," Azinger said to Craig Parry, with whom he was playing that day. At the tenth hole, Azinger holed a fifteen-foot birdie putt by deliberately blading the ball with his sand wedge. "Nice call, Paul," Parry said.

Azinger and putters historically have had a tenuous relationship. The search for a putter that would not betray him led him to use an odd-shaped putter that initially had no name and was dubbed "The Thing." Azinger won the Tour Championship at Pinehurst No. 2 in 1992 using The Thing.

On the eve of the Nissan Open in 1996, Craig Stadler leaned his putter against a table outside the clubhouse and inadvertently left it there. A few minutes before teeing off in the first round the next morning, he realized his putter was missing. He repaired to his locker, where two days earlier a representative of Kevin Burns Golf had left a KB 9304 putter for him to try. "I pulled it out and said, 'Well, this will do,'" Stadler said. "It wasn't grotesquely ugly or anything." By Sunday afternoon, the KB putter had grown on him and was adopted into his family of clubs. He won the tournament with that putter and has kept it in play since.

Vijay Singh's caddy, Dave Renwick, is a free spirit who, following an indifferent first round of 71, gave his boss's putter to a boy. "We needed to give it a rest," Renwick said, recalling the cut Singh had missed only a week before. Singh, incidentally, had planned to return the putter to the closet anyway. He obtained a new Titleist Scotty Cameron putter and three days later won the Honda Classic.

Tiger Woods began using a Scottydale model Scotty Cameron putter quite by accident, and it paid immediate dividends. The day before the Las Vegas Invitational began in 1996, Cameron and Titleist's tour rep Larry Watson were loitering by the putting green as Woods worked on his stroke. Woods's instructor, Butch Harmon, asked Cameron whether he had a putter that would help Tiger keep the club face square through impact on three- to six-foot putts.

Cameron had one Scottydale model available and offered it to Woods, who began using it the next day. Four days later, the twenty-year-old Woods had won his first professional tournament. To commemorate the occasion, Cameron produced a limited edition Tiger Woods signature putter, called the Las Vegas Invitational Scottydale Victory Putter. Only 332 were made, one for each stroke Woods took in winning the ninety-hole tournament. The soles of the putters were inscribed with "1996 Las Vegas Invitational Champion Tiger Woods" and "1st PGA Tour Victory." They became immediate collector's items.

Woods's putter, incidentally, became part of a controversy a few weeks later. Woods avoided a playoff at the Walt Disney World/Oldsmobile Classic when Taylor Smith was disqualified for using a putter with an illegal grip, leaving Woods alone atop the leader board. However, television viewers began calling the United States Golf Association to see whether Woods's putter, in fact, was illegal as well. They thought the hosel of the putter might have been more than five inches in length, in violation of rule 4-1b in the USGA *Rules of Golf*.

David Eger, vice president/competition for the PGA Tour at the time, ruled the putter legal after checking it with calipers prior to the Tour Championship the following week. Unbeknown to Eger, though, Woods had changed putters, replacing the Scottydale with a shiny finish—which had bothered him—with another Scottydale with a dull finish. A Titleist spokesman said the putters were identical, save for the finish.

Smith, incidentally, donated his own putter to Christopher Reeves's charity for spinal-cord injury research, and the putter earned $5,000 for it in an auction. "At least something good came out of it," Smith said.

Players occasionally spend their own money on equipment, though not on the black market. At the Doral-Ryder Open one year, a man stole $15,000 worth of Orlimar woods from the equipment trailer compound, then commandeered a cart that he drove through the hotel parking lot and to the hotel spa. There, he encountered Raymond Floyd, a PGA Tour star who went unrecognized by the thief. The thief then attempted to sell the clubs to Floyd, who informed a security guard, leading to the man's arrest.

"I read a book about America's stupidest criminals," Scott Smith, director of security at the Doral Resort, said. "He has to be one of them."

Jay Delsing said that he once saw Steve Pate enter a pro shop, buy a putter, and then go out and put on a putting clinic, holing everything with it.

Ben Crenshaw is among the best putters in history, yet even he finds reason to punish his putter. A dry spell in 1997 sent him to a golf shop, where he found an old Spalding HBA putter, circa 1960s, in a barrel. He paid $25 for it and put it into play at the GTE Byron Nelson Classic.

In 1999, Stewart began the year without a club contract. Rather than carrying a bag advertising a product for which he was not paid, he went to an Edwin Watts Golf Shop near his home in Orlando, Florida, and purchased one.

"A hundred thirty bucks I spent on this bag," he said. "It's nice, really nice. Edwin Watts on Turkey Lake Road, right by the Kmart. And I shop there, too. I'm really happy with it. If a sponsor does come along, I prefer them to put their name on this bag, because this is a really nice bag. Great pockets."

Stewart, incidentally, never wore his trademark knickers and tam-o'-shanter during practice rounds, and this tended to conceal his identity. Few recognized him out of uniform. He had arrived for a practice round at the Phoenix Open a week earlier wearing slacks and a baseball-style cap and carrying a generic black golf bag. He was stopped at the entrance by a marshal who suspected that Stewart was an interloper crashing the gate.

Technology packaged in an unfamiliar way is a tough sell on tour, but occasionally these clubs get a test that they pass. PRGR developed such a club, one it calls the Zoom, a hybrid of a long iron and a wood that looks like neither. A PRGR rep gave one to Brandel Chamblee, who was not a victim of love at first sight. "It's ugly the first time you see it," he said, "but when you hit it, it gets much prettier. The first time I hit it, it went straight up in the air about two hundred thirty yards, which is not a shot I have, but I have it now."

The worst players, from a tour rep's perspective, are those who are married to their equipment and take theirs vows seriously, notably till death do us part.

Joey Sindelar is among them. "I'm not a club changer," he said. "I never ever, ever, ever, ever, ever . . . rarely change clubs. I go years and years with the same clubs. I'll change wedges, but only to the exact same wedge because the grooves wear out. Putters, I've used two in my whole career, three maybe, although I might throw another putter in the bag for the pro-am, just to make the other one jealous and nervous. Sometimes that works."

Justin Leonard and Davis Love III clung stubbornly to their persimmon drivers, the last in golf to do so. Only reluctantly did they surrender to technology, each eventually putting a Titleist 975D titanium driver in his bag.

Players often change clubs because one endorsement deal is expiring and another is offered by a competing manufacturer. The better players are enticed to switch companies by offers that can reach $1 million or more per year. This has not always proved prudent for them. Payne Stewart used traditional forged blades his entire career before signing a lucrative endorsement contract with Spalding. Offset cavity-back irons proved a difficult adjustment for Stewart, who eventually worked with Spalding club designers on a new set of blade irons that were not offset.

Mark Brooks abandoned his Hogan irons and signed an endorsement contract with Callaway, then went into a prolonged slump. Eventually, he chose to end the agreement with Callaway.

After finishing fourth on the PGA Tour money list in 1996, Steve Stricker signed a new endorsement deal to use Taylor Made clubs, then finished one-hundred-thirtieth the following year. "It's got to be me," he said. "The clubs are fine." He was right. He finished thirteenth on the money list with the same clubs the following year.

3

PRACTICE MAKES . . . MONEY

Tuesday of tournament week is a day for practice rounds, though how this is defined varies. There are those, for instance, who make a *practice* of injecting gambling into their Tuesday *rounds*. The upshot is that some of the more spirited, competitive golf of the week is played before an unsuspecting audience.

Professional golf ordinarily is a game of gentility, governed by rules of etiquette during tournament rounds on Thursday through Sunday, but the dignity with which it is played on those days is replaced by ribald gamesmanship during the Tuesday practice round. The sums for which the golfers play—tens, hundreds, and occasionally thousands of dollars—are miniscule compared with the millions paid out each Sunday, yet those rounds on which they play for their own money often, for some, are more animated, even more enjoyable, however insignificant to the golf world at large.

The games and the stakes vary, but $100 seems to be a popular number among the more rabid bettors on tour. They might play $100 skins, where each hole is worth $100, with the money carrying over to the next hole when no one wins a hole outright. This was the format adopted by television when it created the Thanksgiving-weekend mainstay, The Skins Game, save for one notable difference: the players there aren't playing for their own money, which greatly diminishes the drama.

A more popular game during Tuesday practice rounds, often played for $100, is the Nassau with one-down automatic presses.

This is a game of one-on-one, where each player risks the stipulated sum on three separate bets, payable to the winner of the front nine holes, the back nine holes, and the full eighteen. The stakes rise considerably with the one-down automatic press, because a new bet begins each time a player falls one hole down on a bet.

Then there is the Hammer, an especially spirited game, one that ought to be avoided by the squeamish or those short on capital. When a player hits a poor shot, his opponent can hammer him, which doubles the bet on that hole, provided the player accepts the challenge. Should the player decline to accept the challenge, he forfeits the hole, losing only the original bet. A hammered player who hits a good recovery shot then has the option of returning the hammer, doubling the bet yet again. Moreover, the player who trails in the match has the option of pressing the bet at the outset of any hole, doubling the value of the remaining holes.

The needle exchange that fuels each player's resolve in these friendly but fiercely contested matches had been decidedly one-sided on one particular day, when Phil Mickelson and Paul Azinger were engaged in a game of $25 Hammers. Mickelson was giving and Azinger was receiving. The scene was the Olympic Club in Daly City, California, two days before the start of the Tour Championship there in 1993.

Mickelson was $400 ahead going into the eighteenth hole, which as a result of the bet having been pressed twice was worth $100. Each player drove his ball into the fairway. As they walked toward their balls, Mickelson was taking trash talk to another level, particularly for golf.

"I was really on him, giving him a hard time, roughing him up pretty good," Mickelson said.

Mickelson was first to play and hit an excellent second shot, ten feet beneath the hole, creating an opportunity to make another birdie. Azinger followed with an unremarkable approach that came up short of the green, settling into the deep rough and leaving him with an exceedingly difficult chip shot.

"Well, obviously I'm going to hammer you," a confident and beaming Mickelson said.

"I'm not going to take it," Azinger said flatly, declining to accept the challenge and risk losing $200 on the hole and running his debt to $600.

"That's just what I thought you'd do," Mickelson said, turning up the volume on his abuse in a brazen attempt to shame Azinger into changing his mind.

"I started in on him and was really roughing him up," Mickelson recalled.

Azinger then addressed his ball and was ready to hit the shot. Mickelson's challenge, however, resonated in Azinger's mind, sparking his competitive nature. Finally, he stepped away from his ball, looked at Mickelson, and said tersely, "You're on." Now playing the hole for $200, Azinger readdressed his ball and then stunningly holed the difficult chip for birdie, as a dazed Mickelson looked on, suddenly deflated.

Did Azinger return the verbal assault at that point?

"You *think*?" Mickelson said. "If you thought the celebration at the Ryder Cup was bad, you should have seen this celebration. It was about two minutes later before I finally putted."

"You know what's coming now, don't you?" Azinger finally said needlessly. "I'm hammering you."

Azinger's hammer doubled the bet again, making the eighteenth hole worth $400. Mickelson then carefully lined up his putt, put a firm stroke on the ball, and watched it slide by the hole, a costly miss that resulted in no money exchanging hands for the day, much to Mickelson's chagrin. His was the loser's mien, as Azinger returned the abuse to which he had been subjected much of the day.

Payback is hell.

This particular match represented just another practice round on the PGA Tour. Each Tuesday (and Wednesday at major championships), players play practice rounds to familiarize themselves with the nuances of the course. In the process, they often introduce games of chance to their routines to inject purpose, or at least interest, into these practice sessions on courses they already know by rote from having played them in previous years. "It makes three-foot putts meaningful and gets you focused," Blaine McCallister said.

These games are more likely to be played at major championships than other tournaments, when players already familiar with the course sometimes arrive only in time to play in the pro-am on Wednesday. For the majors (which do not have pro-ams), they typically arrive Sunday night or Monday morning, giving themselves three days of practice rounds and the opportunity to participate in games of chance.

Gambling, of course, is prohibited by the PGA Tour. Its guide, *Player Handbook and Tournament Regulations,* under Conduct of Players, states that players shall not "gamble or play cards on the premises where a PGA Tour cosponsored or coordinated tournament is being played."

Players routinely flout this rule every Tuesday of tournament week and will defend themselves by invoking the time-honored sentiment that gambling is an inherent part of golf. Even the staid United States Golf Association deems gambling permissible. The USGA's *Rules of Golf* has a section entitled "USGA Policy on Gambling," which notes that it "does not object to participation in wagering among individual golfers when participation . . . is limited to the players [and] the players may only wager on themselves or their teams . . . and the primary purpose is the playing of the game for enjoyment."

Enjoyment is open to interpretation. The great sportswriter

Grantland Rice wrote, "A man's true colors will surface quicker in a five-dollar Nassau than in any other form of peacetime diversion that I can name."

"It makes you more competitive," Lanny Wadkins, one of the most passionate money players in golf, once told *Golf World* magazine. Prior to the Ryder Cup in 1993, Wadkins suggested that the U.S. captain, Tom Watson, require his players to play $50 one-down automatic presses (a new bet beginning each time a player falls one hole down on a bet) in practice rounds. "If a guy says it's against his religion," Wadkins said, "tell him to get another religion."

Wadkins is an inveterate golf gambler, who shot a 61 at Shoal Creek prior to a PGA Championship, a 62 at Canterbury prior to another PGA Championship, and a 63 at Merion prior to a U.S. Open, each time with his own money on the line. Rick Reilly of *Sports Illustrated* dubbed him Mr. Tuesday. "For Tuesday," he wrote, "is the day when PGA Tour players play for their own money, and nobody gets a bull neck up faster than Wadkins when his own fresh simoleons are on the line."

He and Tom Watson used to boast that as practice-round teammates they'd never lost a money match. Paul Azinger and Phil Mickelson took this as a challenge. Prior to the Masters in 1994, Mickelson and Azinger engaged Watson and Wadkins in a friendly Nassau. Mickelson birdied the final four holes to produce a victory that ended the streak. Wadkins was spotted on the practice tee later, paying his debt.

Former PGA Tour player Jim Simons was seldom fortunate enough to appear on the receiving end of a bet with Wadkins. The two were teammates at Wake Forest, and one year it was said that Wadkins never lost to Simons, consistently beating him by a stroke. "If I made six bucks off Simons I could eat at McDonald's for lunch and the chicken place for dinner," Wadkins said. "That was my existence."

Wadkins is among those who deem it a requirement to have a vested interest in his own performance in any practice round. So is Arnold Palmer. The frugal Sam Snead often paid off losing bets with a check, assuming correctly that many foes would not cash the check, preferring instead to retain it as a keepsake with the legendary Snead's signature. Tiger Woods, at four, was admonished by his father for putting for quarters.

Gambling is an inherent part of the game.

"No Bogey" is a game occasionally played during practice rounds at major championships. Each player antes a stipulated amount, say $100, and remains in the game until he makes a bogey. The last player who has not made a bogey is declared the winner. On a difficult U.S. Open layout, where a bogey lurks at every turn, this requires a player to focus on every practice-round shot in an effort to remain alive.

A variation of the game was played by Tom Watson, Fred Couples, Mark Calcavecchia, and Lanny Wadkins prior to the British Open at Muirfield one year. The bet was this: Should any player complete eighteen holes without making a bogey, the others would pay him fifteen hundred pounds each. Watson was the only one who did. "He made six- and seven-footers like they were six and seven inches," Couples said.

"You have to have a shot of testosterone in the morning before you play with some of those guys," Peter Jacobsen told *Golf World*. "Lanny would make six birdies on the front nine at Oakmont Tuesday at the Open, and you can't even hit a green. He'd say, 'Well, you're already down nine-eight-seven-six-five-three-and-one on the front, so you owe me eighteen hundred dollars.'"

Professional golf has its legendary gamblers and gambling stories. Raymond Floyd and Lee Trevino belong to the former category and have contributed to the latter. In 1965, a young Floyd, already an accomplished PGA Tour player who recently had won the St. Paul Open, was approached by a renowned hustler, Titanic Thompson, who asked whether he was familiar with a player from El Paso, Texas, named Lee Trevino.

No, Floyd replied, he'd never heard of him. Thompson wondered whether Floyd would engage him for a sum of cash at Trevino's home course, El Paso Country Club.

"In those days," Floyd said, "I'd play anybody I never heard of, even on their own course."

So Floyd traveled to El Paso. The first day, Floyd shot a 65 and Trevino beat him with a 63. The following day, Floyd posted a 64 and Trevino topped him again with a 63.

"Would you like to play him on another course?" Thompson asked.

"No," Floyd replied. "I'm not going to change courses now. I think I can beat him."

On the third and final day the stakes were double or nothing. They arrived at the par-5 eighteenth hole tied and each reached the green in two shots. Floyd made his eighteen-foot eagle putt and Trevino lipped out his fifteen-footer for eagle and lost by a shot. "I don't know how that putt didn't go in," Floyd said.

Floyd finished with a 63 to Trevino's 64, enabling Floyd to leave town with the money he had brought.

"I've never tried to speak Spanish before," Floyd said to Trevino when it was time to depart, "but *adios.*"

Trevino sharpened his gambling skills at Tenison Park, a muny course in East Dallas inhabited by sharks. He recalled a popular game there called "Trees." For every tree you hit, you paid the other player $10. The course featured a plethora of pecan trees, which often reacted in the manner of pinball bumpers that could quickly run up the debt of a player hitting an errant shot.

Floyd also prefers to have a vested interest in his practice rounds, as do Phil Mickelson and Mark Calcavecchia. "I've thought about this," Mickelson said. "If you're in Las Vegas and playing in the casino, that's gambling. I consider golf wagering a form of competition. We're all competitors. When you enter a tournament, you pay an entry fee [of $100]. This is the same thing." Said Calcavecchia, "If I get out there and just play I can't concentrate. But if I've got a match with Phil, I'm going through my routine, the same as I would on the course. Otherwise, I don't care."

Calcavecchia recalled one memorable (or regrettable) high-stakes match he played with Mickelson, even citing the date. "June 12, 1995," he said. "My birthday." It was a practice round prior to the start of the U.S. Open at Shinnecock Hills on Long Island, New York. "That was the day my putter left me," Calcavecchia said. In the course of that practice round, on typical Open greens, hard and fast, Calcavecchia missed six four-foot putts and lost a thousand dollars. "And I've putted like crap ever since," he said. "I was all messed up."

He has better memories of a practice round on the Plantation Course at Kapalua in Maui, Hawaii, prior to the Kapalua International. He was joined by Mike Hulbert, Andy Bean, Ken Green, and four other players, eight total, each playing a $100 Nassau with one-down automatic presses against each other player. "That was the ultimate," Calcavecchia said, noting that he had an exceedingly long piece of paper on which to keep track of the action. Eight players, all playing one another, add up to twenty-eight $100 Nassaus going on at once, each with one-down automatic presses, creating several more layers of bets. "Wild," Calcavecchia said. "Each of us had our own cart and we're all hauling ass down the hill on the first hole, everybody playing everyone else, guys hitting at the same time. We played in three and a half hours. I remember playing the last hole and I made a twelve-foot putt to win $5,000."

Augusta National in the days leading to the start of another Masters is akin to a casino, and stakes are sometimes high, in contrast to the sums for which the club's well-heeled members usually play. The small, friendly wager at Augusta National is common among the members, some of whom find it unseemly to play for larger stakes. Often told is the story—perhaps apocryphal, but entertaining, nevertheless—of how Jackson Stephens, the former chairman of the Masters, once became annoyed by a guest's incessant badgering over the diminutive size of the stakes, both on the course and in a postround game of gin rummy. Finally, Stephens, whose own net worth was in the hundreds of millions, asked the man what his net worth was.

"Ten million dollars," the man allegedly said.

"I'll tell you what," Stephens was said to have replied. "Let's cut the cards for your entire net worth."

One memorable Masters tune-up match actually occurred the Saturday before, at Isleworth Country Club in Windermere, Florida, in 1997. Twenty-one-year-old Tiger Woods and his neighbor and friend Mark O'Meara played a casual round during which Woods shot a course-record 59 that resulted in a $65 payday.

"It could have been a lot more than that," O'Meara said. "Tiger could have shot 56 or 57 that day. I didn't play that well. I just got smart and stopped pressing him."

Eight days later, Woods won the Masters by twelve strokes.

Woods and O'Meara frequently engage in friendly wagers, typically $5 Nassaus, with automatic one-down presses. It is not about the money, obviously, given the wherewithal of the two players.

O'Meara kiddingly suggested that Woods should be obligated to give him strokes. "Look, we can't keep playing these practice rounds in front of all those fans if you're going to hit it sixty or seventy yards by me," O'Meara told him. "On the par-fives, you've got to give me a stroke. You're hitting an 8-iron and I'm hitting a 3-wood." He also noted his age, forty-one at the time, or nineteen years Woods's senior.

When O'Meara won the Masters in 1998, his first major championship, Woods attempted to put an end to this talk of getting strokes. "That's it," he told his friend. "Now that you're champion you need to give me strokes."

"I don't think so, Tiger," O'Meara replied. "But nice try."

The fact is that O'Meara often beats Woods, who precisely a year later lost $100 to his friend in a match at Isleworth in the week leading to the Masters.

"I can't believe you always beat me," Woods said, reaching for his wallet.

"Somebody's got to do it," O'Meara replied. "Not everybody can."

O'Meara in fact beat Woods at the AT&T Pebble Beach National Pro-Am in 1997 (they finished one-two), at the British Open in 1998 (Woods missed joining O'Meara and Brian Watts in a playoff by one stroke), and at the World Match Play Championship in 1998 (in the final).

Early on, Woods was said to have had that affliction commonly known as a reach impediment. His hand failed to reach his pocket to extract payment. "I've got to work on that a little bit," O'Meara said, grinning. "He's young. He's got to learn. Fast pay makes fast friends."

In fact, Woods usually paid as punctually as his means allowed. At Stanford, Woods and his teammate Conrad Ray engaged two other teammates, Casey Martin and Notah Begay III, in a spirited putting contest. Eventually, Woods owed Martin $80, which the latter never expected to see, since students typically lack the capital to pay off debts. Woods figured he could eliminate the debt in another putting contest with Martin, who this time won $100, running Woods's debt to $180. Two days later, Woods presented Martin with a check for $180. Martin retained a photocopy of the check for posterity.

Jack Nicklaus and Arnold Palmer frequently team up at the Masters in an attempt to fleece a pair of youngsters. Brad Faxon noted on his website that he and his friend Billy Andrade teamed in a nine-holer versus the legends, made seven birdies, and "got 'em," Faxon said. "They didn't pay, but that's OK." When Woods was twenty and still an amateur, he played a money game with

Jack Nicklaus and Arnold Palmer on the eve of the Masters at Augusta National and lost. "Arnold won all the money today, not Tiger," Nicklaus said. "I was more impressed with Arnold."

Prior to the Masters in 1999, John Huston and David Duval were engaged in a Nassau at Augusta National that proved costly to the latter. Huston is capable of producing birdies in clusters, as his tour record 28 under par for four rounds in winning the United Airlines Hawaiian Open in 1998 will attest. Of course, Augusta as it is set up for the Masters is somewhat more difficult than the Waialae Country Club in Honolulu. Still, Huston went out in a strong 3-under-par 33 at Augusta, then found his stride, closing with a 29 that included birdies on the final six holes for a round of 62. Numerous presses enabled Huston to defeat Duval ten ways, and, given that hundred-dollar Nassaus are not unusual on the PGA Tour, well, do the math. Duval took a bath.

Huston, moreover, had an even more lucrative day, for he and Mickelson teamed against Duval and John Daly. Mickelson shot 69 and he and Huston produced a better-ball score of 59 that ran the table.

Tim Herron hooked up with David Duval to play "a little money game" with Fuzzy Zoeller and John Daly at Augusta in Herron's first visit there. "I don't want to say how much we played for," Herron recorded in a Masters diary he wrote for the *Minneapolis Star Tribune*, "but let's just say that I paid for the lesson. When I gave Fuzzy the check, I put 'Masters lesson' down in the corner of the check."

Even the par-3 tournament at Augusta produces its share of wagering. Arnold Palmer and Fuzzy Zoeller engaged in a game of thousand-dollar whipout for holes in one, which made it unlikely that money would change hands. When Zoeller aced the ninth hole with a 9-iron, however, Palmer whipped from his pocket a wad of bills held together with a rubber band and peeled off ten hundreds and handed them to Zoeller.

Paul Goydos inadvertently found himself playing a practice round with Arnold Palmer at Augusta National and partnered with him in losing a $5 Nassau to Fred Funk and Woody Austin. Palmer relayed to Goydos a story from a practice round in 1958, when he played a match with Ben Hogan, from whom he won $35. Afterward, the notoriously oblivious Hogan wondered aloud, "How'd that guy get invited to this tournament?" Hogan apparently was unaware that Palmer already was professional golf's newest superstar and the tour's leading money winner to that point of the season.

An unknown club pro, Wayne DeFrancesco, wound up in a practice round with Mark O'Meara, David Duval, and John Cook prior to the PGA Championship at Medinah, and, of course, money exchanged hands. Duval chose DeFrancesco as his partner and the two of them made twelve birdies, eight by Duval. Alas, O'Meara and Cook trumped them, and when O'Meara birdied the final two holes, Duval and DeFrancesco were out $10 apiece. "That's pretty low greens fees to play in that group," DeFrancesco told the *Washington Times*.

A real estate investor and developer and amateur golfer once teamed with Funk to skin Palmer and Nicklaus in a Masters practice round. Ken Bakst had earned a Masters invitation by winning the U.S. Mid-Amateur championship, then received a congratulatory letter from Nicklaus, who invited him to join him in a Tuesday practice round. Then a letter from Palmer arrived, proposing the same thing. The stakes were not revealed, but the game was a Nassau, the crowd was large, and Bakst and Funk won.

Mickelson enjoys a game of chance, however it manifests itself. An avid skier, he once broke his leg by skiing too aggressively early in a new season, costing him a couple of months on the disabled list. At the Western Open one year, he was putting poorly, a fact not lost on his friend Gary McCord, the CBS broadcaster. When Mickelson arrived at the sixteenth green, the television tower there was occupied by a confident McCord, who bet Mickelson $20 that he'd miss his eighteen-foot putt for birdie. Mickelson accepted and then made the putt. From atop the tower, McCord paid by floating a twenty to the ground.

"Ever since then I look for him," Mickelson said, "because I feel like it's a good omen for me. But inside ten feet he doesn't go for it."

Greg Norman admits having gambled to support himself in the days when he worked as an assistant club pro for $28 a week in Australia. He too enjoys games of chance. At the PGA Championship at Riviera one year, he was seen betting his caddy Tony Navarro that he could hit a 2-iron over the forty-foot netting at the opposite end of the range, two hundred forty yards away. Norman won.

Patrick Burke recalled a money game he played with Kevin Sutherland and Steve Rintoul, the latter falling behind and growing increasingly frustrated, particularly with the incessant needling. "We got Steve so mad by the fifteenth hole," Burke said, "that he threw his club so far he couldn't find it. We told him he gets to throw a provisional."

4

THE LONGEST DAY

A staple of tournament golf is the pro-am, always played on Wednesday, on the eve of the tournament, and it is the longest, least enjoyable day of the week for the professionals. Pro-ams are a long, slow, tortuous walk through a minefield, where errant TopFlites struck low, crooked, and hard home in on unsuspecting targets, courageous spectators crowding the rope line, attempting to secure a better view. Golf and boxing have the lethal hook and scoring by rounds in common, but they also share the barbarian act of spilling blood.

"The worst I saw," Phil Mickelson said, "was at Colonial, the tenth hole. There's a bunker on the front left and the pin was back right. This guy had a long bunker shot. He caught it thin and it sailed head high across the green and tagged somebody in the gallery so hard—hit him just above the eye—that the ball came all the way back across the green and into the same bunker, fifty, sixty yards. Amazing. Blood everywhere. It was not good. But I'm sure there have been worse."

The ingredients for a bloodbath are in abundance on pro-am day: bad golfers and large crowds. Hockey star Wayne Gretzky told about hitting a rope hook into the gallery once and beaning a secret service agent following former president Gerald Ford. In the Canadian Open pro-am one year, Gretzky duck-hooked his tee shot at the first hole and knocked out a boy of sixteen, who broke a couple of fingers attempting to deflect the shot in the manner of a goaltender.

Hale Irwin was hit between the eyes during the pro-am at the Los Angeles Open one year, the victim of an errant tee shot hit by an amateur, Rich Saul, the center for the Los Angeles Rams at the time. An ostentatious bandage and a headache notwithstanding, Irwin opened the tournament with rounds of 70 and 67 and was in contention through to the end.

At least those standing in the line of fire do so with emergency help standing by. An amateur in the Greater Hartford Open pro-am one year hit his ball beneath an ambulance in the parking lot. "They had to move it so that he could hit the shot," the pro in the group, Kenny Knox, said. "I thought when he got there he might just climb in."

One Wednesday morning, Mark Calcavecchia was asked whether he had a favorite pro-am story. "I might have a new one in the next five hours," he said. "Every Wednesday is an adventure, let me tell you."

Players endure pro-ams because they are the lifeblood of their tour; each week they generate hundreds of thousands of dollars and a similar measure of goodwill. Typically each pro is paired with three "chops," as unskilled amateurs often are called, who often have ponied up a few thousand dollars for the privilege, unless they've been invited to lend their household name to the marquee.

Celebrities from the sports world are ubiquitous in tour pro-ams and typically have polished games, since their own sports are seasonal, leaving them with several months of free time to work on their golf. An exception was National Basketball Association star Charles Barkley, once a moderately accomplished golfer who arrived at the 1999 Bob Hope Chrysler Classic with a swing that seemingly had been invaded by a virus, causing a spasm prior to impact. Barkley took the club back OK, but when he began his downswing the ugliness began. He paused in mid-downswing, then lunged at the ball, sending it screeching in any direction but the intended one, frequently low right. "Low right is just not good," Phil Mickelson said, shaking his head, concerned that fans in the line of fire have so little time to react and protect themselves.

"He's got a horrible swing, awful, one of the worst I've ever seen, and I've told him that face to chest," said the diminutive former U.S. Open champion Corey Pavin, one of Barkley's playing partners at the Hope, which has four days of pro-am play, conducted in conjunction with the official tournament.

John Daly played with Barkley one day, too, and attempted to correct his flaws, "that break-dance move of his on his backswing," Daly said. Payne Stewart was another of Barkley's playing partners in a group that also included Michael Jordan, who was forced to endure this horrific swing for four consecutive days. "Payne," Jordan said, "I've got to watch for four days, but I don't want you watching. Just turn your head when Charles is swinging."

"Charles," Stewart said, turning to Barkley, "how long has it been like this?"

"Six months," Barkley said.

"I would have quit by now," Stewart replied.

Later, Stewart was asked how his day went playing with Barkley. "I don't think he hit anybody today," Stewart said. "So that's a good thing. He has the flinches. He starts it down and he stops on his downswing and his legs go like this and it's ugly."

Perhaps he was preoccupied. Barkley actually signed his NBA contract near the tenth green, which slowed play considerably, much to the chagrin of the retired legend Michael Jordan.

"Hey, man," Barkley said in response to Jordan's impatience. "Some of us still got jobs."

Jordan had accepted the invitation to play in the Hope only when the tournament agreed to his two requests: that he not have to conduct interviews and that he not be paired with any undesirables. Did Barkley's presence in his foursome represent a breach of promise?

Peter Jacobsen, the quintessential pro-am player and a perennial partner of Jack Lemmon's at the AT&T Pebble Beach National Pro-Am, also had the dubious honor of playing a round with Barkley at the Hope.

"Jack Lemmon is Tiger Woods compared to Charles Barkley," Jacobsen said when asked to compare the two. "Charles has got a hitch or something in his swing. Did you see him on TV? He takes it back, makes a nice turn, starts down, and then he stops and just kind of throws at it. He said someone a couple of years ago gave him a lesson and told him to pause at the top of his swing. And he says it's messed him all up. He was actually a really good player. I played with him when he shot in the mid-70s, low 80s. Now he can't get it airborne. Michael Jordan loves that. He beats him out of a lot of money, and he loves to give Charles the needle. That needle was out all day. And his practice swing is perfect. It's great. It's the way he used to swing the club. Now he does some crazy thing. And I felt so bad for him because he's dying out there."

Larry Barber, who caddied for his friend Gary McCord at the Hope and was in the group behind Barkley, watched in wonderment at the faith the gallery put in this swing gone awry. People lined the fairway ropes, point-blank range for a man with no idea where his ball was headed. "You couldn't pay me enough to stand there," Barber said.

"Sir Charles, it's good to have him back on the court," Mickelson said a week later, when the NBA strike had ended and players had returned to work. Alas, basketball no longer can be counted on to keep Barkley off the tee and away from participating in pro-ams. A knee injury forced him to retire.

Mickelson once was brought down by a Hall of Fame linebacker participating in the Hope. His playing partners were Lawrence Taylor, Mike Ditka, and Joe Pesci, and he had a birdie putt that was important to the team score, never mind what it meant to his individual score. Mickelson hit what seemed to be a perfect putt, the ball homing in on the hole, when suddenly from nowhere another ball rolled across his line and collided with his ball, knocking it off its path.

The culprit was Taylor, who was oblivious of the golf tournament being played around him and was practicing while Mickelson was putting. Mickelson was required to hit the putt again and missed. "That's golf," Mickelson said diplomatically, or at least prudently, given that any anger he might have mustered would have to have been directed at one of the most menacing linebackers in history. "I wasn't going to fight him."

Celebrities from the entertainment industry often have reasonably proficient games as well. When the rock star Alice Cooper quit drinking, he required an addictive pastime to fill the hours once occupied by drinking and the ensuing hangover. He took up golf. "As bad habits go," he said, "an even trade-off." He now plays to a six handicap, endorses Callaway clubs, and, on those occasions when he leaves a putt short, must endure from the gallery a chorus of that shopworn phrase, "Hey, Alice, does your husband play, too?"

The most celebrity-laden pro-am fields are those at the AT&T Pebble Beach National Pro-Am and the Bob Hope Chrysler Classic, each of them started by a world-renowned entertainer hooked on golf. Bing Crosby was the first, inviting his friends from the golf and entertainment industries for an annual clambake now known as the AT&T. His road partner, Hope, followed suit, lending his name to a Palm Springs tournament in 1965.

"The Bob Hope is kind of like an extended cocktail party," Jacobsen said, explaining how the two tournaments differ. "There are cocktail parties going on on the left side of the fairway and on the right side of the fairway. People run back and forth from one party to the other, with extra hotdog buns or mustard, and you're trying to play over the top of it. At Pebble Beach it's real golf. I love the Bob Hope. I play there every year. I've won the tournament. But it's more of a party atmosphere. You're more concerned about whether you have any onion dip over there and or clam dip over here and I'll be right over."

The convergence of golf stars, movie stars, and sports stars generates enormous crowds and creates gridlock, as it did at the AT&T in 1999, when Tiger Woods's partner was Kevin Costner and Mark O'Meara's partner was Ken Griffey Jr., and the four of them played together.

Worse yet was the Bob Hope Chrysler Classic the year it decided to bring the presidents, present and past, together in 1995. President Bill Clinton was joined by former presidents George Bush and Gerald Ford, the three of them teaming with the defending champion Scott Hoch and tournament host Bob Hope in an endurance test at Indian Wells Country Club. Clinton carried nineteen clubs in his bag, five more than allowed by the Rules of Golf. Presumably he was given a presidential pardon for the infraction.

The presidents played bipartisan golf, spraying shots to the liberal and conservative sides of the fairways, left and right.

The round began with Bush hitting a wild second shot that struck a woman in the bridge of the nose, a wound requiring ten stitches. It neared a merciful end when Ford hit a woman at the seventeenth hole, splitting her finger. Clinton afterward called it "the worst round of golf I've played in a long time," invoking a tiresome cliché amateur golfers use in an attempt to convince strangers they're better players than they demonstrated.

Hoch played what ought to be regarded as one of the finest rounds in PGA Tour history, a two-under-par 70 with more commotion than eight years of presidential scandal produced. "That's the best tee to green I've ever seen," Clinton said. "Scott deserved to be ten under par, and he would have been if he hadn't been playing with three politicians who were distracting him and Bob Hope doing a soft-shoe."

Incidentally, Bush, according to a source close to the tournament, had agreed to participate only after he was assured he would not have to play with Clinton, a man who not only differed philosophically from him and had taken his job, but who also is not a kindred spirit in golf. Clinton plays at a painfully slow pace, and Bush prefers to play quickly. The latter reportedly did not have a good time on this extraordinarily long day—five hours, forty minutes of golf. "The longest day," Hoch called it—and has vowed not to return.

Clinton has made no such promises. A devotee of the game and one certain to miss the spotlight once his tenure in office has ended, Clinton figures to turn up in any pro-am that will have him.

"I love to play," he told Hope prior to teeing off. "I like it for the same reason most people dislike it. I like it because it takes so long. I need six holes before I stop thinking about everything going on."

So here's a man with nineteen clubs in his bag, who prefers laboriously slow rounds, and takes mulligans, none of it likely to endear him to the United States Golf Association, which isn't likely to ask him to film any of its "for the good of the game" commercial spots.

Ford, a resident of Rancho Mirage and an avid golfer, is a perennial participant in the Hope. On the par-3 third hole at the Arnold Palmer Private Course at PGA West one year, Ford pushed his tee shot far right of the hole. His ball took one hop and landed in a cardboard trash bin, settling into the rubbish. Ford asked his playing partner, Arnold Palmer, for a ruling. "Can't I just lift the bucket onto the green?" Ford asked.

"You ought to get a new Cadillac or something for making a hole in one," Palmer replied. "I'll just put a 1 on the scorecard."

Instead, Ford discarded his dignity and began riffling through the trash in search of his ball. He found it, took a free drop, then scuffed his chip shot, moving it a scant four feet.

"I should have left it in the bucket," he said disconsolately.

The Bob Hope Chrysler Classic is played on four different courses, though they aren't the same four every year. This can get confusing at times, even for those involved in the production of the tournament. Bob Hope typically plays a few holes to open the first round, though one year he arrived late at the first tee at Indian Wells Country Club. His driver got the Indian part right, but erred on the rest of the equation. Hope was taken to Indian Ridge Country Club, which had been part of the rotation the previous three years but was excluded in 1998. Hope was twenty minutes late for his tee time, causing tournament officials to permit other groups to start ahead of his.

Hope always plays with the defending champion in the first round. In 1994 that was Tom Kite, who nearly paid a bloody price for the privilege. After Hope hit his tee shot, Kite began walking down the fairway. Oblivious and no longer visually acute, Hope decided to hit a mulligan. He pushed a low line drive, sending the ball on a collision course with Kite's head. Fortunately, the ball sailed past Kite with only a few inches to spare.

Players wish to avoid the celebrity field at the Hope, though the greater their name recognition the less likely they are to be so fortunate. Players nonetheless enjoy coming to the California desert in January. The weather typically is perfect, and the golf courses are immaculate, leading to low scoring, even the lowest scoring. David Duval shot a 59 in the final round on the Palmer Course at PGA West to win the tournament in 1999, and Tom Kite once won by shooting 35 under par over five rounds.

The pro-am partnership of Peter Jacobsen and Jack Lemmon is an enduring as well as an endearing one in golf circles. They perennially hook up at the AT&T Pebble Beach National Pro-Am, renewing their quest to play well enough that Lemmon makes the cut for the first time. They aren't necessarily a formidable team, but at least they're an entertaining one.

On one particular hole at the AT&T in 1999, Lemmon asked Jacobsen what club he was hitting.

"I'm hitting a 5-iron," Jacobsen said.

"I'd better hit a 4-iron then," Lemmon replied.

"Jack," Jacobsen said, "9-iron, 4-iron, 4-wood, it doesn't matter. At your age, they all go the same distance anyway."

By now, Lemmon and Jacobsen are fast friends and something of an odd couple. Lemmon annually has to endure Jacobsen's persistent needle, however good-natured.

"Jack knows exactly when to take off his rain suit," Jacobsen said, launching into his favorite Lemmon stories. "He'll wear his rain suit head to toe zipped up to the neck, but when the TV cameras are coming on, he'll take the rain suit off and display this beautiful peach outfit, or canary yellow, or rust. Then no sooner do we play one hole than he'll catch one in the fairway, when it's wet and sloppy, and hit three inches fat and hit it maybe eight or nine yards and he'll have spots of mud all over him the rest of the day, looking like a spotted leopard, mud all over him from head to toe.

"We were playing one year at Cypress Point, Greg Norman, Clint Eastwood, Lemmon, and myself, at the famous par-three sixteenth hole. Norman and I hit 3-woods onto the green and Eastwood and Lemmon decided to lay up, except that Lemmon hit a little slice and the ball hung up in the ice plant over by the cliff, forty or fifty feet down, certain death and dismemberment. Jack said, 'Let it go,' but Clint in his best Dirty Harry voice said, 'You can't let that thing go. You've got to hit that ball.' So Jack started inching his way down the ice plant. I'm thinking this is dangerous. I said, 'Clint, you can't let that happen.' He said, 'Don't worry, I'll hang onto him.' So Eastwood grabbed the back of Lemmon's belt. Then I walked up behind Eastwood and grabbed the back of his belt, and Norman walked up and grabbed the back of my belt. We had this human chain of safety. Then Lemmon took this big swing and the ball came out beautifully on the fairway and the crowd went crazy. Jack pumped his fist. We pulled him out. Then he had sixty yards to the green and what did he do? He shanked the ball back into the ice plant.

"First tee at Cypress one year and we were all nervous. The crowd was lining the right side of the tee. They introduced him, Jack Lemmon from Beverly Hills, California. He then took a big swing and the club went right under the ball, which traveled only about eight yards, *over* the gallery to the right, like an eight-yard punt, and some woman caught it. She didn't know what to do, and then Lemmon yelled, 'Throw it, for God's sake!' She turned and threw it on across the road into the first fairway.

"I remember one year it looked like we were going to make the cut. We came to the eighteenth green and thought we needed a birdie to make it, and I had a forty-footer. Jack was standing there looking glum and I rapped that thing and Fluff [Cowan, Jacobsen's caddy] was tending the pin and the ball went right in the middle of the hole. Lemmon leaped in the air and he was straddling me, his arms wrapped around me. It was unbelievable. He had tears of joy.

"We missed the cut by one. I would probably give up winning one more time for Jack Lemmon to make the cut. I love him like a father."

The standard PGA Tour pro-am is a one-day affair, Wednesdays, and participation by PGA Tour players is a requirement. Typically, one pro is paired with three or four amateurs, usually in a best-ball format. The amateurs run the gamut in ability, though the number of errant shots seems to suggest that the great preponderance of them are mid-handicappers, at best.

Hugh Royer was playing in the Nike Tour Championship pro-am one year when the rough was particularly severe, especially for amateurs tending to hit their ball there. Royer's partner lost twenty-eight balls, or more than three balls every two holes.

Bob Verdi once wrote in *Golf World* magazine about "all those amateurs hitting all those patios in regulation."

If only that's all they hit.

The auto-racing star Jeff Gordon was playing with Amy Grant and Vince Gill in the Bob Hope Chrysler Classic one year. Gordon skulled a shot over the green at the third hole at Indian Wells Country Club. The ball struck a spectator in the forehead, splitting it wide open and spilling blood. The man, incidentally, refused treatment, choosing instead to remain by the green, an inviting target for more bad golf.

Vince Gill may not have raised any welts, but he raised suspicions at the AT&T. "I don't know how Vince pretends to be playing off a one or two handicap, or whatever he's playing off of," Payne Stewart said. "Because if he posted the scores he's shooting it would be way up there. I mean, he is not finishing some of these holes. It's crazy. He's a good player when he's swinging at the ball right, but right now he's not swinging at it very good."

A celebrity with whom Stewart was impressed was actor Samuel L. Jackson. "For someone who's been playing five years, he swings at it pretty nice. He has nice fundamentals in his golf swing."

Jackson, too, has an understanding of golf's dress code. "The golf course," he said, "is the only place I can go dressed like a pimp and fit in perfectly. Anywhere else, lime green pants and alligator shoes, I get a cop on my ass."

When the tennis star Ivan Lendl retired, he turned to golf and became obsessed with the sport and reasonably proficient at it. Yet in one pro-am he hit five balls into a water hazard, which elicited this unsympathetic response from television analyst Roger Maltbie: "Grass isn't his best surface."

Mark O'Meara is an extraordinary pro-am player, his gregarious nature blending perfectly with a format that requires interaction with amateur partners. He has won at Pebble Beach five times and at Disney, another tournament with a pro-am format, once. He also lost in a playoff at the Hope once. Yet even he occasionally gets exasperated with his amateur partners. At the Bob Hope Chrysler Classic one year, O'Meara had a five-footer for par at the seventeenth hole. One of his amateur partners had a four-foot bogey putt for net par.

"Mark, do you mind if I go ahead and go first?" the amateur asked. "If I make this, that's a 5 for a net 4, just in case you miss yours."

"Go ahead," O'Meara said reluctantly.

When they were through putting out, O'Meara's caddy, Jerry Higginbotham, politely set the record straight with the amateur.

"Listen, this is what my man does for a living," Higginbotham said. "Don't be feeding him negative vibes."

O'Meara took exception once to the plethora of golf carts driven by those in the gallery at the Hope. Members of the respective country clubs sometimes follow the action in their private golf carts, violating tournament rules. Several drove up to the tee box at the thirteenth hole at La Quinta Country Club one year, just as O'Meara was about to tee off. Distracted, he pull-hooked his shot out of bounds.

"Two members in carts parked right behind the ropes," O'Meara said after the round. "That's fine if you're just having a beer and playing around out here. I didn't say anything, because if I say something it's going to seem like, 'Here's a pro complaining again.' But this isn't a college tournament. It isn't an amateur tournament. It isn't the shootout on men's stag day. It's a professional tournament. This is how I make my living. It's a very tough game, and it takes a lot of concentration, and a lot of money is at stake. I was pretty hot. I would think it might have had something to do with my poor tee shot, but I didn't blame them. I hit the shot. I just want people to understand. I don't know if they really care, truthfully."

O'Meara still shot a 66, but the tee shot and the resultant penalty proved costly; ultimately he lost the tournament in a play-off with Corey Pavin.

Wednesday pro-ams needn't be entirely a waste of the players' time, provided they tap into the wisdom of those with whom they have an opportunity to play. The middle class is virtually priced out of pro-ams, which carry entry fees upwards of $3,000. Fields are filled primarily with those who have achieved financial success, including businessmen with vast reservoirs of business and financial knowledge. Joe Ogilvie has an economics degree from Duke and is an active player in the stock market, particularly the technology sector. Ogilvie attempts to arrange as his pro-am partners chief executive officers of companies in which he might be interested from an investment perspective. "That's the reason I love playing in pro-ams," he said. "I like to bounce ideas off those guys."

Mark O'Meara figured this angle out years ago. He frequently played in the AT&T as the partner of Bob Allen, chairman of the company sponsoring the tournament. Jack Welch of General Electric and Bob McCurry of Toyota also are friends on whom he can lean for advice. "If I have a business decision to make and need advice, why not ask some of the most successful business guys in the world?" O'Meara wrote in a *Golf World* magazine piece entitled, "Why I Love Pro-Ams." "I'm not afraid to call up Bob Allen of AT&T and ask him what he thinks, because we have developed a friendship. Golf is the outlet to put you in touch with business."

Or even with beer salesmen. Patrick Burke once was paired with Joseph Coors, heir to the brewing empire, who announced that he'd give Burke a six-pack if he were to make a ten-foot putt for eagle at the seventeenth hole. "Make it a case," Burke said. Coors agreed and Burke holed the pressure putt. "He still owes me a case," Burke said.

Wayne Levi readily admits that he plays professional golf for the money and follows the stock market avidly. He too enjoys the pro-ams for the information that can be culled from them. "You're around a lot of influential people," he said. "You can talk business."

One of the more unexpected, though perhaps not undeserved, pro-am moments in recent memory occurred off the course, at the pro-am party on the eve of the final CVS Charity Classic, a family-run tournament in Sutton, Massachusetts, that died after thirty-two years, when the PGA Tour declined to accommodate its request for an autumn date.

The tournament's executive director Ted Mingolla addressed the audience and announced that the G and A in PGA Tour "stood for 'greed' and 'arrogance.'" Two of the PGA Tour's members, Billy Andrade and Brad Faxon, each of them hailing from the Northeast, stepped up and became cohosts of the new CVS Charity Classic, which no longer is an official PGA Tour event but continues to raise substantial sums for charity.

The sandbagger—the man claiming a considerably higher handicap than his ability reveals he should have—occasionally infiltrates the pro-am, tipping the odds unfairly in his favor. When he does so at the AT&T Pebble Beach National Pro-Am, he stands out more than Bill Murray in his green tam-o'-shanter with the small flagstick protruding from it. Fred Couples once had Kansas City Royals star George Brett as his partner at Pebble Beach, and Brett displayed a Hall of Fame swing—from the left side, of course—that defied the fourteen-handicap he was claiming. They won the pro-am, raising suspicions in the process.

A more celebrated recent case was that of actor Andy Garcia, claiming a fourteen United States Golf Association index, and helping his partner, Paul Stankowski, by thirty-two strokes. They, too, won the pro-am. A *Golf World* headline called it "an Oscar-winning performance."

"I don't care what anybody says," Garcia said. "I'm not a sand-bagger."

The tournament apparently did not agree. The following year, it knocked his handicap down to an eleven.

This brings to mind the case of Masashi Yamada, a Japanese amateur who helped his pro partner, Bruce Vaughan, by forty-five shots and delivered a victory in the pro-am at Pebble Beach. Yamada was found to have falsified his handicap and was stripped of the victory by AT&T officials.

This served to point out one more similarity golf has with boxing. Occasionally the fix is in.

5

THE WAITING GAME

They are vultures of sorts, though not by choice. They would prefer to be in the tournament field, obviously, but even being out is sometimes better than the limbo in which they exist, often until the last group tees off to begin the tournament on Thursday. They are neither in nor out, instead suspended in between, standing by quietly, waiting for their prey to drop.

"Billy Ray Brown, he was watching me like a hawk," Skip Kendall said, invoking the wrong bird, but the right image during the Players Championship in 1999. On the eve of the tournament, Kendall had wrenched his back, ending his practice round after a single hole. He recovered sufficiently to begin play on Thursday, and another alternate, in this case Brown, went home without having made a swing in earnest.

These are the alternates. They reside in golf's purgatory, awaiting an opening into that week's event. The tournament field is set the previous Friday, the deadline for entering. The number of those who wish to play exceeds available spots, requiring that fields be established according to players' standing in the hierarchy known as the priority ranking, determined by a convoluted formula based on past performance. Those lower on the list who wish to play but don't make the field become alternates, whose entry into the tournament depends on someone's withdrawing prior to the scheduled tee time on Thursday.

Off-course management is critical to the alternate, who has to decide whether to expend the money and energy to travel to a tournament site, a costly gamble that often proves a loser. The trip frequently is for naught. The most graphic example of the plight of the alternate was a photograph in *Golf World* on the day the U.S. Open began at the Olympic Club in 1998. Michael Allen, the first alternate, was laid out on a bench near the practice tee, asleep, his caddy and golf bag a few feet away at the ready. The wakeup call never came; no one withdrew and Allen's trip there was wasted. He went home.

"When you're an alternate you feel like a third-rate citizen," Brown told the *Columbus Dispatch*, as he was awaiting a spot to open in the Memorial one year. "The guys you play with every day, all of a sudden you're not one of them, even though you are. You sit there and think, 'Do I even belong in this locker room with these guys? Should I even be here?' It's like you're an outcast."

The alternate has to remain close to a phone and ready to go at a moment's notice. "It's tough," R.W. Eaks said, "because you're kind of on call. You've got to be mentally ready to play at all times."

Steve Hart had barely a moment's notice at the U.S. Open in 1997. He was staying at a private home and was brushing his teeth at 6:10 on the morning of the first round, when the phone rang. A United States Golf Association official was calling to inform him that Brad Bryant had withdrawn, opening a spot for Hart provided he could make a 7 a.m. tee time. He of course accepted, shaved quickly and carelessly, drawing blood in the process, dressed, and was at the Congressional Country Club in time to hit a handful of balls before reporting to the first tee. He shot a 74.

In 1991, John Daly elected to remain home in Memphis, Tennessee, the week of the PGA Championship at Crooked Stick Golf Club in Carmel, Indiana, outside Indianapolis. An obscure country boy originally from Dardanelle, Arkansas, Daly was the ninth alternate and unlikely to get into the field. The first alternate generally has a decent chance, but the odds decrease dramatically beyond that, particularly at major championships. Yet by Tuesday, five players had withdrawn, moving Daly up to fourth on the alternate list. The three players ahead of him ultimately decided against making the trek to Indianapolis, gauging their chance of yet another player's withdrawing as remote.

At 5 p.m. on Wednesday, Daly began the seven-and-a-half hour drive from Memphis to Indianapolis. When he arrived after midnight, a message awaited him, informing him that Nick Price had been summoned home to Florida, where his pregnant wife had gone into labor. Daly was in the field.

The eleventh-hour call denied him the luxury of a practice round on a long, difficult course with which he was not familiar. He at least employed a caddy who had been around the course. Jeff "Squeeky" Medlin, Price's caddy, had agreed to loop for Daly, who opened the tournament with a respectable 69 that generated virtually no attention.

A 67 in the second round enabled Daly to move up the leader board, and his standing in concert with his towering tee shots began to attract interest. By Saturday afternoon, the golf world was giddy at the prospect that this hard-hitting, obscure hayseed would win the PGA Championship. He shot another 69 and opened a three-stroke lead, then closed with a 71 for a three-stroke victory that was as improbable as any in the history of major championships.

It was more than a victory for the ages, though. It too was a triumph for the vultures, the alternates stuck in limbo, standing by helplessly, in the manner of the neglected one in a game of pick-up basketball. With that victory, Daly became their role model, the beau ideal of the alternates.

Typically, those high on the alternate list are standing by at the tournament site, practicing as though they're in the field, meanwhile casting a wary eye over its players. It is unseemly to root against another in this sport of gentility, so the alternate watches pragmatically, aware that this game that so readily inflicts back pain might do so to a degree that causes a player to withdraw.

"I asked someone if he had seen Jeff Gillooly lately, because I needed him to take care of about four guys for me," said Barry Cheesman, jokingly. Cheesman was an alternate at the Memorial in Dublin, Ohio, and was invoking the name of skater Tonya Harding's ex-husband and one-time "hit man," the man who rapped Nancy Kerrigan in the knee weeks before the Winter Olympics in 1994.

The role of the alternate is one capable of exacting a price, notably the cost of a full-fare coach airline ticket and a hotel room. Kelly Gibson began as the ninth alternate at the PGA Championship at Valhalla Golf Club in Louisville in 1996. He weighed the chances that enough players would withdraw to grant him entry and concluded he might as well remain at home in New Orleans. A day before the tournament began, he had moved up to second alternate and made the hard decision to take a chance, traveling from New Orleans to Louisville.

Gibson must have concluded he was playing the starring role in the film *The Out of Towners*. His flight was delayed two hours. When he finally arrived and went to the baggage claim, he discovered his golf bag had been damaged. When he arrived at the hotel, he was informed that his reservation apparently had been lost.

Still, he found a room, slept for three hours, and went to the golf course, uncertain about his status. More than twelve hours later, the final group teed off, without another player's withdrawing, ending Gibson's bid to join the field. A rain delay meant that he had missed his flight home, forcing him to stay an extra day. All in all, he was out $2,000 with nothing to show in return.

Rex Caldwell was home in San Antonio when he got the call that the Greater Hartford Open had a spot for him. The call, however, came only two days before the event began, which would have required that Caldwell purchase a full-fare coach airline ticket, at $1,200. "I can't afford that," he said, citing a familiar lament of the alternate set. "I live month to month, like all Americans."

Australia's Robert Allenby once fared even worse. Since he was not in the field at the lucrative Players Championship in Ponte Vedra, Florida, he flew from New Orleans home to Melbourne, a twenty-seven-hour journey that began on the Saturday before and got him there on Monday of tournament week. At 3:30 a.m. Wednesday, his phone rang; it was a PGA Tour official calling to inform him that as a result of withdrawals a spot had opened for him in the field. The $3.5 million purse was too substantial for Allenby to take a pass. He booked a flight for 3:45 p.m. that afternoon, which would enable him to arrive in Florida Wednesday evening, in time for his Thursday morning tee time.

Later that morning, he learned his flight actually left at 1 p.m. He hastily arranged to take a helicopter to the Melbourne airport and eventually arrived at the gate at 1:05 p.m., only to learn that the flight was delayed by an hour. Finally, he arrived in Jacksonville at 3:30 a.m. Thursday, thirty-two hours after leaving Melbourne. Allenby ended up shooting 75–71 and missing the cut, giving him nothing to show but rather substantial expenses.

Mike Reid once was the last alternate at the PGA Championship. His bid to secure a place in the field was so remote that he was on the phone arranging a flight home when John Mahaffey withdrew fifteen minutes before his tee time. Reid had time to hit about ten range balls before reporting to the first tee. He had no game balls of his own. A Maxfli representative riffled through his box and produced a couple of sleeves of balls that had been prepared for Jack Nicklaus and had been imprinted with "Jack."

Reid, incidentally, had been without a courtesy car; alternates aren't provided one. The legendary Byron Nelson had had one and had left town early, so Reid inherited Lord Byron's car to go with the Golden Bear's golf balls, a gilded duo whose magic failed to transfer to Reid. He missed the cut.

The alternate sometimes is placed in an awkward position over which he has no control. Australia's Bradley Hughes was a victim once. At the Honda Classic, he was so far down the alternate list that he never bothered asking the PGA Tour for a release to play in the Portuguese Open on the European Tour. A PGA Tour release is required when a player forgoes a tour event to play overseas, unless the player's position on the priority list precludes him from gaining entry into the tour event that week. Hughes had played in the Moroccan Open and had traveled to Portugal, when the PGA Tour called. "About eleven people withdrew on Monday," Hughes explained. "So I had to fly back from Portugal to play and I got here Wednesday and just did no good at all. I had no choice. Because I didn't ask for a release to play away from the PGA Tour, I couldn't play [in Portugal]. I had to either not play at all or come back here [to the Honda]." He called it "one of the crazier rules." Who could argue otherwise?

Taylor Smith, the sixth alternate, experienced the worst way to gain entry into a tournament. He got into the PGA Championship at Winged Foot in 1997 when Corey Pavin withdrew after his father suffered a fatal heart attack.

"My wife and I both broke down in tears when we found out," Smith said.

Smith arrived having missed six of his last seven cuts, yet he opened with rounds of 71 and 71 to qualify for weekend play, and ultimately finished in a tie for fifty-third, earning him $5,280.

It might have been a pittance, as tournament purses go, but it was better than nothing, the take-home pay of the losers of the tour's waiting game.

6

MEN AT PLAY

Tee times on the PGA Tour are not assigned arbitrarily—not entirely, anyway. When Mark O'Meara saw that he was joining the sundowners Thursday in the first round of the PGA Championship at Medinah outside Chicago in 1999, he suspected trouble lurking in the shadows.

"I must be in the penalty box," he said of his 2:28 p.m. tee time. His was the third to last group going off, followed only by obscure club pros last in the pecking order.

O'Meara's tee time seemed to be his penance for having been the first to raise the issue of Ryder Cup pay with PGA of America's chief executive officer Jim Awtrey two years earlier. During the next two years, O'Meara had continued to be outspoken on behalf of remuneration for players. His insistence that players ought to get paid had created an enduring and expanding controversy that threatened to undermine the sanctity of an event thought to have been above reproach. Historically, Ryder Cup players received only a token stipend to cover expenses. Their reward was the opportunity to represent their country. When the Ryder Cup grew in stature and become wildly popular with the public, it began generating massive profits for the PGA of America. O'Meara spearheaded the campaign to persuade the PGA of America to share it with the players, even pleading his case publicly.

Though O'Meara's late tee time might not have been an act of vengeance on the PGA's part, it smacked of one. Undoubtedly, the hierarchy at the PGA of America was not amused by O'Meara's Ryder Cup stance or by the fact that he aired it publicly.

So there he was, playing through the shadows. "I was out there picking up flagsticks," O'Meara said, jokingly referring to the superintendent's job of collecting the flagsticks to prevent their theft after the final group of the day plays through on each hole.

There is a pecking order on the PGA Tour, which ranks players on the basis of their accomplishments and pairs them accordingly over the first two rounds of a tournament. Even Tiger Woods had to climb the ranks. In his professional debut in 1996, he played in the Greater Milwaukee Open on a sponsor's invitation, a three-time U.S. Amateur champion with $43 million in endorsement contracts, paired with two obscure tour players, Jeff Hart and John Elliott. Of course, there was an Augusta-sized crowd lining both sides of the fairway, surely the largest ever to witness a group from the lowest rung of the PGA Tour ladder. Woods's initial shot as a professional traveled three hundred thirty-six yards, the first indication that it would not be a methodical climb up the ladder.

The tour places players in one of four categories for the purpose of pairing them in the first two rounds of a tournament. Each pairing receives one morning and one afternoon tee time, though the higher the category the less likely a golfer is to be subjected to the outer limits of either tee time group.

O'Meara falls into Category 1, which includes tournament winners within the previous three calendar years and the top twenty-five players on the money list the previous year. Category 1A includes those who have won tournaments, but not in the three previous calendar years. Category 2 includes players currently in the top one hundred twenty-five on the money list, those with $500,000 or more in official career earnings, and world-class foreign players who are not members of the PGA Tour. Category 3 includes all others, who typically are assigned the latest or earliest tee times in the first round.

The ignominious tee time he received at Medinah would not have been assigned to O'Meara either a week earlier or a week later. The PGA Championship, however, does not fall under the jurisdiction of the PGA Tour, even though the tour counts it as one of its events. The PGA of America, the club pro division of professional golf, operates the PGA Championship and can determine the pairings as it sees fit, though it usually follows the PGA Tour parameters reasonably closely.

So there was O'Meara, the winner of the Masters and the British Open the previous year, one of the preeminent players in golf, teeing off in the doghouse.

"I saw some of the guys in the locker room and they said, 'How'd you do?'" O'Meara said. "I told them, 'I'm just going out.' Twenty guys must have come up to me and said, 'Nice tee time.' I was warming up and the club pros were saying, 'What are you doing here?'"

It stood to reason that O'Meara would deduce that his late tee time was a form of punishment administered by an angry PGA of America.

The United States Golf Association pairs the defending champion with the reigning U.S. Amateur and British Open champions in the first two rounds of the U.S. Open. This put the Amateur champion Tiger Woods in a pairing with the British Open champion John Daly and the defending champion Corey Pavin at Oakland Hills in 1996, a long-drive contest at which the short-hitting Pavin was merely a spectator.

Of course, this was not a unique development. At the Open a year earlier, Pavin was paired in the first two rounds with Vijay Singh and Davis Love III, each of them a long hitter. "Needless to say," Pavin said, "the most common phrase was 'Corey, you're away.'"

The USGA otherwise pairs arbitrarily and occasionally takes liberties to ensure an attractive pairing or a nostalgic one, as it did for the '94 Open at Oakmont. It assigned Jack Nicklaus to play with Arnold Palmer in remembrance of their historic playoff at the Open in 1962.

The Masters pairs the defending champion with the reigning U.S. Amateur champion in the first round, but beyond that assigns its times arbitrarily.

This is how John Daly came to be paired with Ian Woosnam in the first round of the Masters in 1994. By virtue of their similar scores, they were paired again in the second, third, and fourth rounds as well. "Woosie and I were talking marriage," said Daly, who has had three wives. "It's the longest relationship I've ever had."

Even the PGA Tour occasionally comes under suspicion for curious pairings, although a computer that considers only the four categories determines its pairings. In 1996, Scott Hoch skipped the British Open and subsequently was criticized publicly by two PGA Tour players, Davis Love III and Brad Faxon, who questioned why an American star would elect not to play in one of golf's most prestigious tournaments. Instead, Hoch played in the Deposit Guaranty Classic in Madison, Mississippi, where he responded to his critics. "I don't care what they think," he said. "Golf is not a team game." A few weeks later, Hoch and his vocal critics all were playing in the Sprint International and were paired together in the first two rounds. The tour claimed that this was a coincidence. Hoch called it a strange coincidence.

"The tour said it's done by computer at the office," Hoch said. "I said, 'OK, but who programs the computer?'"

Hoch might have been surprised to find Faxon and Love at the first tee at the Sprint, but he would not have been surprised to encounter Susan Naylor there, or on the first tee of any other stop on the PGA Tour. Naylor (or an associate) is a fixture on the first tee in the first round of every PGA Tour event. Naylor co-owns the

Darrell Survey, regarded in the equipment industry as the J. D. Power of golf.

When the players, or more precisely their golf bags, arrive at the first or tenth tee (depending on where they start their rounds; the tour uses both) on Thursday morning, a Darrell Survey rep is there to poke around in each bag, charting the player's equipment by category: driver, fairway woods, irons, wedges, putter, shafts, and ball. The company even charts a player's shoes, spikes, and clothes.

The Darrell Survey numbers are not taken lightly, either. The information is used as a weapon in the battlefield of equipment sales. The numbers show a manufacturer's tour presence—the number of players using its equipment. Orlimar Golf often cited Darrell Survey numbers in its advertising, while Callaway Golf contended that Orlimar was deliberately misusing the numbers to mislead the public. Callaway sued Orlimar as a result. Orlimar filed a countersuit. This is serious business.

Naylor sells the information she gathers and does not readily share it with those who want it gratis. When Justin Leonard moved to the first tee at Congressional Country Club at the U.S. Open in 1997, a man with a black badge sidled over to Naylor and her partner and brother John Minkley. He was inquiring about Leonard's driver, one of the few remaining in professional golf that were made of persimmon rather than metal. Mistaking the man for a reporter, Naylor and Minkley declined to reveal the information. The man finally identified himself as a secret service agent sent by President Clinton, who was curious about the implement used by Leonard a week before in winning the Kemper Open.

"That's cool," Leonard said. "The president wants my driver. We can work out a deal."

The Darrell Survey was started in 1934 by Eddie Darrell, who called himself the Sherlock of the Shankers, given the fact that he was often required to snoop to obtain accurate information. Players historically have attempted to evade the truth. The Titleist revolution in golf balls in the '30s enticed players to use the ball they endorsed only on the first hole, then to switch to a Titleist for the remainder of the round (before the *Rules of Golf* were amended to include the one-brand rule). This was designed to deceive Darrell into recording that they were playing the ball for which they were paid, to appease those writing the checks. The rotund Darrell quickly caught on to this ploy. When he suspected a switch was coming, he'd hide in the trees near the second fairway. When the player hit his tee shot, Darrell would sprint—to the degree that he could—onto the fairway to inspect the ball.

"There were a lot of shenanigans going on," the pro Ed Furgol said.

The shenanigans still go on, though not at the frequency they once did. Naylor recalled a player approaching her and asking what she had written down for his driver. She told him.

"No, that's not what I have," he said.

"But I just looked in the bag," Naylor said. "It was right there."

"That's wrong, that's absolutely wrong. I want you to write the other name down."

The solution? "Eddie used to say, 'Always have an eraser. You can't start a fight on the tee,'" Naylor said. The information could be corrected later.

What the public sees from afar sometimes conceals the truth, which is why Darrell Survey reps will pull head-covers off woods to inspect the brand. One player won an event and its $1 million purse using a driver of a brand other than the one for which he was being paid, though he at least concealed it beneath the proper head-cover. The Darrell Survey rep peeked beneath the head-cover and the information was duly and accurately recorded.

Arnold Palmer is an inveterate tinkerer, a man who won't hesitate to change equipment, even on occasion shelving clubs manufactured by his own company to try a competitor's product. On the first tee of the Masters, he encountered a familiar Darrell Survey rep, as he had on countless occasions over the years. This time he would not permit a peek beneath the head-covers bearing his own company's logo, instead attempting to provide the information verbally, by informing the rep that he had all Palmer woods. Darrel Survey reps are instructed never to accept a player's word at face value, but Palmer is the King and out of deference the Darrel Survey rep acquiesced. Palmer was actually giving an Orlimar fairway wood a trial, a fact he wished to conceal, so he hid it beneath a Palmer head-cover.

Other players periodically attempt to deceive Naylor and by extension the companies they represent. They don't want it known by their benefactors that they're experimenting with a competitor's product. Naylor nonetheless subsists on the accuracy of her information and assiduously checks and double-checks if necessary.

It happens only occasionally, though once on the Senior Tour, Naylor said six of seventy-six players told her they were playing one brand of club and were caught using another brand.

Another time, Naylor's attempt to inspect the make of a player's shoes was met with resistance.

"FootJoys," the player said.

"Oh," Naylor replied, by then having heard it all. "Is FootJoy putting the Etonic logo on its shoes now?"

A player's tournament week begins in earnest on Thursdays, moments after Naylor has obtained her information. A starter introduces each player as his turn to hit from the first tee arrives. The next four days are an endurance test and obstacle course fraught with peril.

Patience is a virtue. A round of professional golf seemingly has redefined a word, **e·ter·ni·ty** (î-tûr′nî-tê) *noun: eighteen holes on the PGA Tour.*

"If a golfer fell off the Empire State Building," the late great sportswriter Jim Murray wrote, "it would take him a week to hit the ground. He would be checking the yardage all the way down."

Or, as Lee Trevino once said of a deliberate playing partner, he could have begun the round clean-shaven and finished it with a beard.

Slow play is a problem that was introduced by Jack Nicklaus, whose methodical play generally has been credited with changing the pace of the game. Future generations of golfers watched Nicklaus on television and were influenced by the deliberate way he prepared to hit a shot, including the seemingly interminable amount of time he stood over the ball before pulling the trigger. Nicklaus's results—seventy PGA Tour victories, eighteen professional major championships—became the justification for future generations of players to go about their business in a similarly deliberate manner. The methodical pre-shot routine became the norm rather than the exception, on or off the PGA Tour.

On the PGA Tour, it was an unwelcome distraction. Nicklaus's rivalry with Arnold Palmer was in its neophyte stage, yet already had been firmly established, creating tension between them. One day Palmer was asked what he thought of the young Nicklaus.

"I think he should play faster," Palmer replied.

The slower players today are similarly reviled by the faster players, who are taken out of their rhythm, creating a mental obstacle to high-quality golf. The potential for a slow-play penalty looms as well; should a group fall behind, each player in the group is susceptible to a slow-play penalty.

At the Nissan Open one year, the group of Don Pooley, Neal Lancaster, and Mark Wiebe received a slow-play warning after falling too far behind the group ahead of them, moving each player to the brink of incurring a penalty. In an attempt to close the gap, Pooley exited the ninth green before Wiebe had finished putting. When Wiebe arrived at the tenth tee, he said tersely to Pooley, "I made my putt." Pooley became angry, and it was reflected in his play. He had birdied the ninth hole and was in contention, but double-bogeyed the twelfth and bogeyed four of the last six holes to shoot 42 on the back nine. He eventually finished sixteenth. "The guy was way out of line," Pooley said later. "He made a comment that changed the momentum of my play."

Perhaps the slowest among the contemporary players was Glen Day, who in recent years has learned to pick up the pace. He once played at such a laboriously slow pace that he acquired an appropriate and obvious nickname: Glen *All* Day. "I've sped up a lot," he said. "That's part of the reason for my success, because I've gotten quicker. The quicker I can make up my mind and hit the shot, the better I'm going to play. But, yes, I was slow, and, yes, I still can be slow. But I'm aware of it and am working on that."

The European Ryder Cup team in 1999 might benefit similarly from a prodding. The team reacted angrily at the premature U.S. celebration at the seventeenth green, after Justin Leonard holed a forty-five-foot putt, but the U.S. team was miffed at what it perceived to be the painstakingly slow pace at which the Europeans played. Ireland's Padraig Harrington was the worst offender. "At times in their singles match," *Golf World* magazine wrote, "he seemed like he was hoping [Mark] O'Meara would retire between shots."

The PGA Tour frowns on slow play and has attempted to address the issue on numerous occasions. Originally, players who fell out of position were warned. On their third warning, they were fined $500 and then $1,000, an insufficient deterrent given the vast amounts of money at stake. Later, a stroke penalty was assessed on the third offense, the stroke representing a considerably greater penalty given the potential consequences in a tournament determined by strokes.

The more deliberate players in recent years have included Germany's Bernhard Langer and Britain's Nick Faldo. Mark O'Meara was paired with Faldo at the Mercedes Championship one year and was threatened with a slow-play penalty. "It wasn't me," O'Meara said later, "and Nick and I were playing together. He told me that he was walking fast between shots, and what I thought was, 'Well, all I know is we're behind, and it takes you forever when you get over the ball.' But I can't tell Nick Faldo, 'Hey, speed up. You're taking too much time to pull the trigger.' When he missed the green with his approach on sixteen, he must have walked back and forth forever."

Early in his tour career, David Duval was painstakingly slow on occasion, as was sarcastically noted by a network television analyst. *Sports Illustrated* wrote that he admitted that "buttoning his shirts all the way to the top is evidence of being 'a little bit anal,' a characteristic that he admits contributes to his being a fastidious, and sometimes annoyingly slow, player."

Tiger Woods was fined $1,000 for slow play at Bay Hill in 1997. "It's going to kill me," he said, sarcasm and a touch of anger dripping from his words.

Jeff Sluman was assessed a $1,000 slow-penalty fine once and protested. He took forty-seven seconds to hit a bunker shot, seven seconds over the allowable limit. His excuse was that the bunker had been poorly maintained, increasing the difficulty in deciding how to play the shot. Colleagues supported him and the PGA Tour eventually rescinded the fine.

Those with broods at home handle slow play best. "It takes a lot of patience," Peter Jacobsen said. "It helps when you've got a bunch of kids at home who drive you nuts."

Brad Faxon lamented slow play in a column he wrote for *Golf World* in 1997. "You used to look at your group to see if you'd be playing with talkers or quiet, serious guys," he wrote. "Now you look to see if they're fast or slow."

Probably the fastest is John Daly, who used to pull a club and hit his shot before his caddy Greg Rita was done calculating the yardage to the hole.

These days, players check to see whether they're playing with Tiger Woods, a blessing whichever way it goes. Weekend pairings are done according to scores, from highest to lowest. Since Woods is virtually always among the lowest, those paired with him probably are in contention. But being paired with Woods also represents a challenge, given his intimidating presence, as well as the massive throngs he attracts. "When you've got Tiger," Paul Goydos said jokingly, "you don't get the wind because the people block it."

Many of those people are not necessarily familiar or concerned with the etiquette of the game, either. Often they are quiet and still only when Woods is hitting; once his shot is airborne, they become tidal waves of humanity, rolling menacingly and relentlessly toward the green or the next tee, while Woods's playing partner is left to attempt to play through the chaos.

Goydos joined Woods once for an early time at the GTE Byron Nelson Classic one year. "I was a little shocked," Goydos said. "You could actually see grass and trees and stuff. I was expecting it to be just a blanket, but by the end of the day it was. The crowd had to have tripled."

This, incidentally, was the first time that Goydos had been paired with Woods. "I think he's got a future," Goydos said.

Rocco Mediate had the unenviable task of playing with Woods in the final round of the Phoenix Open in 1999. At the twelfth green, a man in the gallery said to Woods, "Knock it in, Tiger. If you do, Rocco will fold like a cheap suit."

"Well, that pissed me off," Mediate said later. "I walked over toward him, and I pointed at him and said, 'Really? Will I fold like a cheap suit?' I almost made the putt, and he said it again. I was so mad. It was a stupid thing to say, but it got me going a little bit."

Mediate birdied the next hole en route to his first victory in six years.

"They're doing it because they want to be funny," Mediate said. "They're not doing it because they have a problem with me. They just want Tiger to win, which is how it's going to be. I knew that's how it was going to be. Tiger was great about it. He said many times, 'Don't listen. Just shake it off.'"

The disadvantages of playing with Woods include the fact that he might be the recipient of advantages, as he was in that same round with Mediate. Woods missed a fairway, and his ball came to rest behind an enormous boulder that no one man was capable of moving. The rules permit the moving of loose impediments, of which a rock ostensibly is one. Several men from the gallery helped roll the boulder out of the way, enabling Woods to hit his shot toward the green rather than having to chip back to the fairway.

Nick Faldo, among others, pointed out that though it apparently was legal it was not necessarily in accordance with the spirit of the rule. Moreover, Faldo said, this was an advantage Woods had over another player, who might have nothing more than a couple of guys and a dog following him, and the dog, Faldo said, "might cock his leg at the rock."

PGA Tour players routinely attempt to get relief from a sticky situation, and this was among them. "The first thing that goes through your mind when you're in the trees," Phil Mickelson said, "is are there any burrowing animal holes? A stake attached to the tree? What can I possibly do? You're looking for anthills, whatever. Everything will cross your mind as to what you can possibly do to get relief. On tour we have a hot one, fresh sod. It gets taken to the limit, I think. If you get a bad lie, you say, 'I think this is new sod.' So yes, you're constantly trying. That's the advantage of knowing the rules and using them for your advantage."

The Canadian lefthander Mike Weir had the distinction of playing with Woods in the final round of both the Western Open and the PGA Championship, neither of which worked out to his satisfaction. Woods won them both.

"I knew that people would be pulling for Tiger big-time," Weir said at the Western Open. "I just had to block that out and play my own game. You know, I heard a few fans rooting for me."

How big was his contingent, which included his family?

"Probably eight," he said, laughing. "Plus a few lone Canadians roaming around out there, I think. I saw a few Canadian flags out there."

A month later, at the PGA Championship at Medinah Country Club, Weir took a lead into the final round, shot 80, and was left in Woods's wake. A day earlier, England's Lee Westwood drew Woods and was in ill humor after enduring an afternoon of unruly behavior from the gallery. After shooting a 74 that dropped him down the leader board, Westwood was asked to assess the bright side of his round. "I won't be playing with Tiger tomorrow," he said.

Photographers, those who don't routinely work golf tournaments specifically, also represent a potential problem, though generally only for Woods, their reason for being there. At the eighteenth green at the Riviera Country Club during the first round of the Nissan Open in 1997, Woods stood over a par putt when the staccato beat of a camera's shutter broke his concentration and piqued his anger.

"Why don't you all clear out of here?" his caddy Mike Cowan yelled at the herd of photographers on hand, a blanket denunciation for the error of one. "I don't care who did it. Would you all just move?"

A camera click in midswing is a potential death knell for that particular shot. Woods heard one as he was hitting his tee shot at the eighteenth green in the final round of the Masters in 1997. Though he had an insurmountable lead, he glared in anger at the offending photographer as the ball sailed left of the fairway.

Woods is not alone in reacting negatively to the inappropriate click of a camera's shutter. Davis Love III was in midswing once when the unmistakable sound of a camera distracted him. He turned to a PGA Tour official and asked, "What's the penalty for killing a photographer, one stroke or two?"

An angry Greg Norman confronted a photographer during the second round of the U.S. Open in 1996. The photographer apologized and explained that he had never before been on a golf course and was uncertain why he even had this assignment. Incidentally, he was working for Cobra, the equipment company with whom Norman had an endorsement deal, and the man was there to shoot promotional shots.

Players are easily distracted, some more than others. "Gardner (Dickinson) could hear a mosquito break wind two fairways away," the former CBS producer and director Frank Chirkinian told *Golf Digest*. Colin Montgomerie attempted to redirect an overhead blimp that was distracting him during the U.S. Open at the Olympic Club in Daly City, California.

The golfer's inability to deal with noise is one distinction between his game and other professional sports. Another is that golfers police themselves, tweaking the old saw that defines character as how you act when no one is looking. It is not uncommon for players to assess penalties on themselves, though the infraction was not witnessed by others.

Jeff Sluman disqualified himself at the Bay Hill Invitational in 1996 for committing an infraction no one saw by taking what he later thought might have been an illegal drop. He declined to take bows for sportsmanship, instead invoking an old Bobby Jones line: "It would be like congratulating someone for not robbing a bank."

At the Greater Hartford Open one year, Greg Norman was using a prototype Maxfli ball that already had been approved by the United States Golf Association, but the company had mislabeled the ball. In effect, then, Norman was using a model that had not been approved by the USGA. When he discovered the error, Norman reported it to tour authorities, who informed him that he was disqualified.

"You live by the rules of the game," Norman said, accepting his punishment with dignity.

Love penalized himself at the Western Open in 1994 when he addressed his ball and it moved imperceptibly. This penalty stroke, incidentally, ultimately kept him from finishing among the top thirty money winners, which would have earned him a Masters invitation in 1995. Love later noted that had he not called the penalty on himself and had ultimately won the Masters, the victory would have been tainted in his mind. Love, incidentally, won the Freeport-McMoRan Classic one week before the '95 Masters to earn an invitation anyway.

Arnold Palmer called a penalty on himself when his ball moved at address on the sixth green at Augusta National in 1998, though there were no witnesses. No matter. "I saw it move," Palmer said. The penalty stroke resulted in his taking a quadruple-bogey 7, rather than a triple-bogey 6, which changed his score from 88 to 89. So be it. "I have a free mind now," Palmer said.

"I'm never surprised when it happens," said David Fay, executive director of the USGA, which publishes the *Rules of Golf*. "It's expected. I'd say the players sometimes are surprised that people are surprised."

This is the code of the game, the only sport in which the participants have a responsibility to govern themselves. It is a game of honor, the teacher Harvey Penick wrote. "Observing the customs of honor should be so deeply ingrained that it never occurs to you to play dishonorably."

In 1993, Tom Kite lost the Kemper Open to Grant Waite by a single shot. In the course of the final round, Waite took a drop from an area marked "ground under repair." As he prepared to hit his shot, Kite noticed that Waite's heel was inside the marked area, a two-stroke penalty were he to have hit the shot.

"We don't need any penalties here," Kite said to Waite, informing him of the potential rules violation. Kite's sportsmanship eventually cost him the tournament.

Former Masters champion Larry Mize was in a deep bunker at the Buick Open in Flint, Michigan. Unbeknownst to anyone but himself, he brushed some grass growing in the bunker. "Nobody had seen it," his playing partner Olin Browne said. "Yet he assessed himself a two-shot penalty on the spot. Larry is a class act. I cannot say enough positive things about him."

Justin Leonard stood over a putt that measured ten inches at most at the Canadian Open, a gimme, a tap-in. Yet when he grounded his putter in front of his ball, he saw the ball move, however imperceptibly. He informed his playing partner that he was penalizing himself a stroke.

Tournament officials reviewed a videotape of the incident and were unable to detect movement. They offered to rescind the penalty, but Leonard declined. "What do people think," he said, "that I just wanted to punish myself more? I saw the ball move."

The penalty looms at every turn, and the penalty stroke is the bane of the tour player's existence, to be avoided at all costs.

Steve Elkington once was standing in a hazard, waiting to hit a shot from there, when he mindlessly snatched a couple of blades of grass on which to chew. "Two strokes," he said, when he realized what he had done was taboo in a hazard.

One year Doug Barron lost a ball that landed in the rough right of the eighteenth hole at the Players Championship. More than a dozen people searched for the ball in the area in which it was seen landing and none could find it, resulting in a one-stroke penalty.

John Huston once faced a long downhill putt in the Mercedes Championship at La Costa. Once the ball started rolling, it showed a disinclination to stop. Its momentum took it past the hole and over a slight ridge, propelling down the face of the green and into a pond. He actually found water with a putt, resulting in a dreaded penalty stroke.

Lee Janzen nearly had to take a penalty for losing his ball while tossing it to his caddy Dave Musgrove. Janzen had marked his ball on the green, then tossed it to Musgrove, who was too close to make a clean catch. The ball disappeared, though a spectator said he saw it land in Janzen's bag. A thorough search failed to turn up the ball. However, another man in the gallery claimed to have seen it sail into the bag's ball pocket. This presented another problem: it is a two-stroke penalty if you can't identify your ball. Inasmuch as Janzen's ball had joined similar balls in the ball pocket, how could he identify the ball he had in play? It had grass stains, fortunately.

Phil Mickelson and Brad Faxon were unable to avoid two-stroke penalties for hitting the wrong ball in the second round of the Buick Invitational of California in 1995. They were paired together and each was playing a Titleist 1, though Mickelson was playing a Titleist Professional and Faxon a Titleist Tour Balata. Moreover, each player had put his own distinct marking on the ball to further differentiate them, as all players on the PGA Tour do.

At the tenth hole of the South Course at Torrey Pines, each player hit his ball to the left side of the fairway; the balls ended up only a few feet from each other. The ball Mickelson thought was his had collected mud, obscuring the markings. "I thought my ball was left of his," Mickelson said. "They were only a few yards apart. He played his shot and I played mine."

When they reached the green, each discovered he had played the wrong ball, resulting in a two-stroke penalty for both and a return to the fairway to hit their shots again. Both made double-bogeys.

Nick Faldo was penalized two strokes for hitting Jim McGovern's ball from the rough on the seventeenth hole at Turnberry during the British Open one year.

The British Open champion Paul Lawrie was penalized two strokes when his ball landed in an area marked "ground under repair" and he took the requisite one-club-length relief, then dropped his ball onto the putting surface.

Early in his career, Payne Stewart hit the wrong ball on two separate occasions. Each time, he had hit his shot into the rough; when he arrived, he saw a Titleist and hit it, only to discover later that it had not been his Titleist. Each incident cost him two strokes. After the second time, he invested sixty-nine cents in a Magic Marker, he said, and put a distinguishable mark on his ball.

Stewart once removed an out-of-bounds stake near which his ball had landed. His playing partner informed him his action was not allowed. Stewart replaced it, then hit his shot, all of it too late to avoid the two-stroke penalty for the violation of a rule that says an OB stake cannot be moved.

When he still played a better game than he talked, the Irishman David Feherty once marked his ball with a hotel key, rather than with a coin or some other appropriate ball marker, resulting in a one-stroke penalty for violating Rule 20–1 of the *Rules of Golf*, which states that the ball should be marked with "a ball marker, small coin or other similar object."

"In Britain we have a hexagonal coin, and Egyptian coins can be triangular, so it was a tough call," Feherty said.

Craig Stadler incurred a two-stroke penalty for arriving late for work, although he apparently was on time. At the Mercedes Championship, Stadler had an 8:02 a.m. tee time in the first round. He was there, waiting for starter Bob Fulton to announce him. Fulton failed to see him, a curious oversight in itself, given the fact that Stadler with his girth and bushy mustache does not necessarily blend into a crowd.

At 8:03, Stadler launched his tee shot and played the first hole without introduction. Meanwhile, Fulton informed PGA Tour official Mike Shea that Stadler had been late. Shea caught up with Stadler on the second tee and informed him that he was being penalized two strokes for a late arrival.

"I sat there for two minutes before I teed off," Stadler said. "I was just waiting to be called, as always. Business as usual. Bob's been doing this for umpteen years. He looked at his watch and didn't see me at 8:02." The starter, incidentally, is there in an unofficial capacity and is not required to introduce a player before he tees off.

This was the second unusual penalty incurred by Stadler, who previously was disqualified for putting down a towel to protect his trousers as he kneeled to hit a shot from beneath branches of a tree at Torrey Pines one year. After his latest run-in with the PGA Tour law, he lamented his luck. "Why me? I ought to change my name to (Nancy) Kerrigan."

Taylor Smith had a 7:54 a.m. starting time for the final round of the Shell Houston Open. He slept through four wake-up calls, blew the starting time, and was disqualified.

Rain delayed the Players Championship in 1987. Moments before play resumed, Seve Ballesteros stood on the sixth tee and asked his playing partner, Raymond Floyd, whether it was acceptable to hit a few balls to warm up. Floyd said it was OK, and each of them took a couple of balls from his bag and hit them into the adjacent woods. The result: A two-stroke penalty for each for practicing in an area not designated for that purpose.

The PGA Tour each year mails out letters to its members, informing them of rules changes. One year, it changed its rule on relief from a ball that lands on a cart path from two club lengths to one. Jay Haas failed to read the letter. At the Bob Hope Desert Classic, Haas took relief of two club lengths, then took a drop in an area that had faded white lines, indicating that it was ground under repair. He picked up his ball and moved it. Later, Haas was informed that he was penalized two strokes for taking an illegal drop, one stroke for placing his ball, and two strokes for playing the ball from the wrong place, a total of five penalty strokes in a matter of seconds.

Haas is an affable man who was able to joke about it later. Doing so does not make him unique, but neither does it make him part of a crowd. By and large, players go about their business stoically, without animation or apparent joy. The players who establish a rapport with fans are an endangered species, particularly as Fuzzy Zoeller approaches fifty and the likely end of his PGA Tour career.

"People ask me sometimes, 'Why don't you smile more on the golf course?'" Bobby Wadkins said. "I said, 'You know, I have a great big house at home. I have a kid in a private school. I have a wife who loves to shop. I have to make some money. This is my business. This is what I do for a living. And it's easy to smile when you're shooting 65, but sometimes you're shooting 75 and you're grinding for that last couple of thousand bucks.'"

P.H. Horgan III, a PGA Tour journeyman, was addressing the same subject at the PGA Tour Qualifying Tournament, a grueling six-round affair in which players essentially have their careers at stake. Horgan's fiancée went home early in the event. "She just couldn't take it," Horgan told *Golfweek* magazine. "It is a heck of a way to make a living. I know a lot of fans think of the tour as a bunch of spoiled millionaires waiting around for courtesy cars. But not everyone is Tiger Woods or David Duval. When you're playing well, this is fun. When you aren't, it's really, really tough."

Ken Green, whose personal problems matched his foundering golf game, is a kindred spirit. "When your scores are 75, 76 every day and financially you're going into a hole and your personal life is in a hole, I defy anyone to have fun."

PGA Tour players have the most fun when they use their ability to make a hard game resemble an easy one, and sometimes they are directly rewarded for having done so. It is a tour that finds new ways to further enrich its already well-heeled constituency. On the two-hundred-eighteen-yard par-3 fifth hole at the TPC at River Highlands, site of the Canon Greater Hartford Open, Mark Calcavecchia made a hole in one using a 4-iron. "Hit it just terrible the first four holes," he said. "Didn't hit a good shot. Just got up there and fired. Turned out it was just one of those things, a perfect shot. I'm eightieth on the money list, so this could be the highlight of my year."

His reward? A new Rolex watch.

The hotel valet misplaced Peter Jacobsen's Nissan courtesy car one year at the Nissan Open, so he accepted Johnny Miller's offer of a ride to the Riviera Country Club. On the par-3 fourteenth hole later that day, Jacobsen made a hole in one and won a Nissan 300ZX, a dubious distinction for him and the sponsor. Jacobsen endorses Toyota, which was emblazoned across the front of his visor. Jacobsen at least was savvy enough to recognize the conflict. He tossed aside his visor and hopped into the automobile.

On the same course, in the PGA Championship in 1995, Sweden's Per-Ulrik Johannsen made a rare double eagle that failed to earn him even a modicum of respect from a cocktail waitress that night. "I was in a bar in L.A., when CNN showed the highlight," Johannsen said. "I pointed at the TV and said, 'Look, that's me.' The waitress looked up and said, 'No it's not,' and walked away."

Charles Raulerson also made a double eagle, on the first hole at the Doral-Ryder Open. His wife, Liz, wanted her husband to take the keepsake ball out of play. Raulerson declined, offering the golfer's superstition that since you don't quit playing a birdie ball you shouldn't quit playing a double-eagle ball, either.

Two holes later, Raulerson hit the same ball into a pond. Undeterred and determined to get her keepsake, Liz waded in after it, finally locating it embedded in mud on the bank of the pond.

A ball need not disappear into a hole to be recalled as a momentous one. Early in his professional career, Tiger Woods was attempting to come from behind to catch Mark O'Meara in the final round of the AT&T Pebble Beach National Pro-Am. Woods's tee shot at the famous eighteenth hole there trickled just into the rough on a cold, wet day, leaving him two hundred eighty yards from the green. His playing partner that day was Jesper Parnevik, who previously had confided to friends that Woods was a product of hype, that his skill level did not support it.

Parnevik, meanwhile, hit his second shot and noticed Woods waiting for the green to clear. Parnevik knew there was no way Woods could reach the green from that lie into a slight breeze on a cold, wet day. When the green cleared, Woods pulled a 3-wood, lashed at the ball, and sent it soaring in a high arc toward the green, the ball eventually reaching the front edge.

"It made my hair stand up," Parnevik said, pointing to the hairs on his arm. It was on this shot that Parnevik came to understand that Woods's talent indeed was a match for the hype.

John Daly's length is a dazzling freak show that routinely elicits wonderment from the gallery. In the final round of the BellSouth Classic one year, Daly came to the fourteenth hole, three hundred thirty-five yards long, with a creek bisecting the fairway just short of the green. In each of the previous three rounds, Daly had laid up with an iron. Now he was four shots off the lead and running short of holes. So he pulled his driver, to the delight of the crowd, which emitted a low rumble that reached the green ahead of him. There, Davis Love III was preparing to putt. He turned back toward the tee and said, "He's going to try."

Daly put what he called the "full kill" on the drive. The ball traveled three hundred fifteen yards in the air and landed in the creek, where it bounced off a rock and toward the flagstick. The ball just slid by the hole and stopped fifteen feet away.

Mark Calcavecchia was in the group behind Daly and heard the roar of the crowd.

"What happened, J.D.?" Calcavecchia asked him.

"I just lipped out for a one," Daly replied.

7

THEY DON'T TRAVEL LIGHT

The tour bag contains a variety of pockets in which players can stash whatever they choose, even deceased loved ones. The strangest item ever carried in a tour event surely was Arnie Spence, Scott Spence's father. Scott Spence is a club pro who had qualified to play in the PGA Championship in 1999. He brought along his father's ashes for luck.

"Good old Ziploc," Spence said when asked what kind of container he was using to store dear old dad. "Maybe I can get some endorsements from Glad."

Arnie Spence had died of cancer five months earlier. "He's an inspiration," Spence said during the tournament. "You go through this very difficult game, and you need to have a lot of patience. My dad taught me that."

"It's unusual," he added, regarding the ashes. "But he's part of me. I think I'll go the same route. Hopefully my boys will carry on the tradition. . . . Hopefully not too soon."

The loss of a parent is a burden, one that Spence chose to bring along with him, underscoring the fact that professional golfers do not travel light.

Arnold Palmer is among them. He never is entirely satisfied with his fourteen clubs, the limit allowed by the rules during a competition. Palmer always brings along several extra with which he practices before deciding on the fourteen that make the cut on that specific day.

Larry Guest, a columnist at the *Orlando Sentinel*, once caddied for Palmer for the purpose of writing a magazine piece, and noted that during a practice round, Palmer carried twenty-one clubs, a dozen balls, a sweater, a rain suit, a visor, a hat, an umbrella, spare contact lenses and lubricant, sunblock, energy bars, tees, pencils, a couple of extra golf gloves, bandages, tape, and a jackknife. Total weight: sixty-three pounds.

In the course of a tournament round, players always pack fourteen clubs, though occasionally a player inadvertently has had a fifteenth club in violation of the rules. Tom Watson once had a cut-down iron, extremely short, that belonged to his young son, that had slipped from sight. When the club was discovered, Watson was disqualified.

Various combinations of clubs are used by players to reach fourteen. A typical set is made up of driver and 3-wood, 2-iron through 9-iron, pitching wedge, sand wedge, lob wedge, and putter. Some players—Tom Lehman among them—will carry a 1-iron, and Lehman does not carry a lob wedge.

David Toms knew he had an unusual mix when he carried four woods, including a 7-wood, at the Sprint International. The 7-wood enabled him to hit the ball high, which paid dividends at the par-5 eighth hole at Castle Pines. He used the 7-wood to fly his ball over a stand of trees and onto the green in two shots en route to victory there.

"My bag looks kind of funny with four woods in it," he said. "It looks like I'm a fifteen-handicapper out there playing golf."

When Jesper Parnevik is in contention on Sunday, he probably has a cigar in his bag, though he ordinarily does not smoke cigars. When he won his first PGA Tour event—the Phoenix Open in 1998—he took a three-stroke lead into the final hole. Once he hit his approach shot to the green and winning was imminent, he pulled a cigar from his bag, lit it, and had a victory smoke as he made his way to the eighteenth green.

When he won again, at the 1999 Greater Greensboro Open, he had a tap-in putt left for victory, pulled another cigar from his bag, and lit it. His third victory, at the Bob Hope Chrysler Classic, came while he was on the practice tee, hitting balls in the event that his pursuer, Rory Sabbatini, caught him on the last hole to force a play-off. When Sabbatini's birdie putt slid by, Parnevik pulled from his bag a cheroot that had been given him by one of his pro-am partners, the radio celebrity Rick Dees.

For some players, what they don't carry is notable. The University of Houston has had a strong golf history, counting among its lettermen Fred Couples, Blaine McCallister, Bruce Lietzke, and Steve Elkington. Houston and the University of Texas are golf rivals. McCallister, who played with Couples at Houston, refuses to carry orange tees, orange representing the color of the Texas Longhorns. "I hate Texas," McCallister said.

Jack Nicklaus habitually carries three dimes for use as ball marks and three tees in his pocket. Lee Janzen has copped to carrying a shoehorn. "One time I had to take my shoe off because of a blister or something and couldn't get it back on," he said. "So that's why I put a shoehorn in my bag. I don't like to make the same mistake over and over."

He also carries a roll of toilet paper, though not for the kinds of emergencies it might suggest. "For allergies," he said.

Robert Allenby is said to carry eight pairs of sunglasses, each with a different lens designed for a different light condition.

Virtually all players on the PGA Tour at least passed through college—a few even earned degrees—and the players are generally well read. Tiger Wood leans toward Dean Koontz, who hails from the same part of the world, Orange County, California. David Duval is an aficionado of Ayn Rand's *The Fountainhead*.

But there is one book they all have in common, the best-selling book on the PGA Tour. They carry it to the first tee of every round. Its de facto title: *The Book*. It retails for $12 and is the handiwork of a former caddy, George Lucas, who charts yardages from various places on each hole to the front of the green, helping players calculate exactly how many yards they have to the pin on each shot.

It is a different game from that played by Hogan and Snead and those before them, who essentially eyeballed a green and a flagstick to determine the best club for the job. Jack Nicklaus and Deane Beman ushered in the era of charting golf courses, and today most courses have one-hundred-fifty-yard markers, as well as sprinkler heads that are marked with yardages to the center of greens. At the 2000 Mercedes Championship at Kapalua, when Ernie Els and Tiger Woods dueled down the stretch, Els was sizing up his second shot into the par-5 eighteenth. A sprinkler head he inspected was marked "Dream." It was more than two hundred eighty yards to the front of the green, Els said. "It sounds like a long way, but it can be done. It was downhill and downwind. I still had to hit a good 3-wood to get there."

Lucas takes yardages to another level, charting the distance from bushes and trees and other landmarks, as well as double-checking the courses' own measurements.

Today, nothing is left to chance. Andy Martinez, Tom Lehman's veteran caddy, said *The Book* has been more valuable than even graphite and titanium in reducing scores.

Lucas is so meticulous that he even charts distances from areas a tour player is not likely to hit in. In those places, Lucas provides the yardage with a notation, J.I.C.Y.R.F.U. Just In Case You Really Fucked Up. This is not necessarily what, say, David Duval wishes to see when he is already angry, or, as they say in the peculiar vernacular of the game, when his chili is running hot. But Lucas's editorial comments come with the package. He also adds his artist's renderings of the denizens of the deep, the fish that inhabit the ponds, or the scuba divers hired to collect lost balls.

Players generally know exactly how far they can hit with each club, often by practicing with the use of an expensive laser measuring device many players often take with them to tournaments. If, say, a full 8-iron travels one hundred fifty-five yards with no wind, and the yardage to the pin, calculated by using *The Book* and the pin placement sheet the tour provides players each day, is precisely one hundred fifty-five yards, then there is no guesswork as to which club to use.

A book that many do not carry is *The Rules of Golf*. The Darrell Survey was commissioned by *Golf Digest* to poll a cross section of players on whether they carried one. Of thirty players polled, twenty-two said they did not have a rule book in their bag.

A book that many travel with is the Bible. Dan Bateman travels with the Koran. He converted to Islam in 1994 and eventually changed his first name to Ahmad.

"Golf is like Zen," said Bateman, who met his wife Shinta on the Asian Tour. "The point isn't to do well. The point is to have the right attitude and perspective. Everything comes from that. God and family are infinitely more important than a number next to your name. I can't wait to have a lousy round to test my new attitude."

When former U.S. Open champion Steve Jones was asked about the contents of his bag, he reached into a side pocket and pulled out a photograph of a fish. Jones had caught it on a fly-fishing expedition. Presumably it was too cumbersome to stuff and carry in his bag, so he settled for a snapshot.

All tour pros typically carry a Gor-Tex rain suit in the event that they are caught in a downpour, a sweater to steel themselves against a chill, an umbrella, an extra golf glove or two, sunscreen, lip balm, and an adequate supply of ammunition. They typically change their ball after three holes, though some might go longer, particularly if it has demonstrated the ability to fall when its owner is putting for birdie.

Players have learned to carry Sharpies, as well, using them for autographs. They have learned that it's better to carry your own writing instrument. Otherwise, fans tend to stick pens and pencils at players, occasionally stabbing them. Lee Trevino used to wear a black windbreaker upon exiting the scoring tent, so that he wouldn't become ink-stained.

After winning the British Open, Justin Leonard next teed it up in the Sprint International, at which he was hounded by autograph seekers on Tuesday of that week. "This is the first time I've ever ruined a shirt on Tuesday from autographs," he said, startled by the commotion. "I've heard about it. I've just never seen it."

Tiger Woods was cut under his eye when he was jabbed with a pen at the Phoenix Open one year.

Players carry snack foods, too. Sergio Garcia is likely to pull Power Bars from his bag. Al Geiberger always had a peanut butter sandwich.

The golf balls players carry often are imprinted with a name or a nickname. Tiger Woods's Titleist Professional balls have the imprint "Tiger" on them. Greg Norman's Maxfli balls are labeled "Shark," Craig Stadler's Stratas read "Walrus." Glen Day has his stamped either with "ALL DAY," the nickname he earned early in his career for his lethargic pace of play, or with "Whitney Elizabeth Day" or "Francis Christina Day" in honor of his two daughters. Day also wears, pinned to his hat, buttons with his daughters' photographs on them.

Duffy Waldorf's golf balls are adorned with a variety of artwork courtesy of his wife or kids. At the La Cantera Texas Open, he used balls that had an outline of the state of Texas or a star, symbolic of the Lone Star State. His son Tyler wrote, "You Can Do It, Daddy," on one, and his son Shea drew a snake and armadillo on another. Waldorf won the tournament. He won the Buick Classic at Westchester Country Club in Rye, New York, by playing the last three holes of regulation and one playoff hole with a ball that said, "It's up to you" on one side, and "New York, New York" on the other.

"The golf balls are a really good thing," Waldorf said. "You're out there on the course, you need a kick. You might have made a bad shot, then you see the ball and it says, 'Hang in there, Dad,' and it breaks up your bad thoughts or any bad routines you get into. You can't help but feel better."

It was what Andrew Magee failed to bring with him that revealed his state of mind as he advanced toward the final of the WGC Match Play Championship at La Costa Resort and Spa in Carlsbad, California.

"These are La Costa socks," he said, pointing to his hosiery after winning his quarterfinal match. "Ten bucks, baby. I didn't expect to be here. I packed for the L.A. Open and I packed enough socks, maybe, to get me halfway through this week and then I was going home and have a nice weekend off. But I've got to play now. I'm thrilled about it."

Copper bracelets and magnets have become popular health accoutrements on the PGA Tour.

"This magnet stuff they've come out with is supposed to help pull the arthritis and tendinitis and all this other good stuff out of your body," Fuzzy Zoeller said. "I've been wearing one now for a little over a year and the jury is still out on whether it works or not. I'm still having trouble, but it looks kind of cute, so what the hell, I figure I'd wear it. And another thing. It's free. The key word there was 'free.'"

Bursitis in his left shoulder proved exceedingly bothersome for John Huston, who on the advice of instructor David Leadbetter began to experiment with magnet therapy. Huston invested in a magnetic mattress cover that he takes on the road with him. Huston also has magnets in the soles of his shoes and would rub large magnets on his sore joint. He claims no expertise in the science at work, but swears that since employing magnet therapy the bursitis that he said "was killing me" has been alleviated.

A series of mishaps convinced Steve Pate that he needed help in healing and warding off future mishaps. He fractured his right wrist in an automobile accident, then tripped on a dock and broke his left wrist. For therapeutic purposes, he wears a magnetic bracelet and a copper bracelet on his right wrist.

"And I've got a pint of chicken blood and a voodoo doll in my bag, too, just in case," he said, presumably in jest.

Rich Beem carries for luck his employee card from a previous job that taught him the downside of working for a living. Beem and a friend worked together at the Magnolia Hi-Fi store in Seattle. "Both of us were miserable," Beem said. "Our boss hated us. All the other employees kind of liked us to a point, but our bosses hated us. We had so much fun. It was a joke."

Beem had the employee card with him when he won the Kemper Open, his first PGA Tour victory in his first year on tour. "I will continue to carry the Magnolia Hi-Fi card forever now," he said. He also had brought along his good-luck charm, the friend, David, with whom he sold stereo equipment and portable phones.

J. L. Lewis brings his family along, even during the school year. His kids, Cole and Sherry, are home-schooled by his wife, Dawn. "I got married and had kids because I want to spend time with them," he said. "And we just decided this was the way to do it. So that's our choice. I don't know that it's for everybody, but my wife is a special person and she can handle it. I give them the option every year and say, 'If you want to stay home and go to school you can.' My son likes sports and he's a good athlete and we may put him back in. But they like it out there."

Gabriel Hjertstedt of Sweden brings along his personal trainer, Boris Kuzmic. "It gets more expensive," he said, "but I just want to try to do everything I can to get an edge. And he's really been great. We work out four or five times a week, and that's paying off. I've got energy when I finish my round."

As a result, he too has increased his strength and by extension his distance off the tee. "The last two years," he said, "I've added probably twenty-five yards on my [driving] average."

Beepers are a staple of those whose pregnant wives are closing in on their due dates. Phil Mickelson carried one at the U.S. Open in 1999. The tournament began on June 17 and his wife Amy was pregnant and due to deliver on June 30. He had a private plane standing by and had calculated the time door-to-door (or, rather, course-to-hospital) from Pinehurst, North Carolina, to Scottsdale, Arizona, at five hours, fifteen minutes.

"We've got a little code in case someone calls it accidentally or beeps us accidentally," he said. "If she punches in that code, I'm getting out."

The story took on increased importance as each day passed and Mickelson remained in contention. "If," someone asked following the third round, "the beeper goes off tomorrow while you're . . . "

"I'm out of here," he said, without requiring that the question be finished. "No decisions."

Still, the questions came. "If you are three or four shots ahead with three or four holes to play, do you really think Amy is going to beep you?

"I think if something like that is going to happen there are ways to slow down the labor process. Tributalin is a medicine that calms the muscle contractions. She saw the doctor today. Everything looks great. It's going to be another week or two. I just don't see that happening tomorrow. She's resting, doing everything she can to make sure it doesn't happen. And to hold off one more day, I think that that won't be a problem. If it is and if she does beep me, I know it's serious and it's time to go."

Mickelson eventually lost by a single stroke to Payne Stewart and the beeper did not go off. Had Stewart missed the fifteen-foot par putt he made to win, he and Mickelson would have been in an eighteen-hole playoff the following day, during which Mickelson's beeper would have sounded. Amy went into labor the day after the Open had ended.

Tom Lehman carried a beeper when he brought his two-year-old son to a tournament with him. "I may look like a crack dealer," he said, "but I'm just trying to be a good parent. If there's a crisis at the day-care center while I'm playing they can reach me."

Tiger Woods has a tiger head-cover for his driver, made by his mother Kultida, a native of Thailand, who inscribed on it Thai words that translate as "Love from Mom." Fred Funk said he brings along a broom, which he uses to warm up. "I read a magazine article when I was fourteen that said Sam Snead always swings with a broom and I've been doing that ever since," Funk said.

Billy Mayfair and his wife, Tammy, travel with their two rottweilers, sisters called Tulsa and Dallas, and stay only at pet-friendly hotels, of which the Hilton in Valencia, California, apparently was one. When the Nissan Open moved to Valencia Country Club one year, the dogs were seen each day chasing around the hotel grounds. When Mayfair was playing, they remained in the room with the television on to keep them company. Mayfair, incidentally, won that tournament, and the dogs were dashing about the eighteenth green moments after their master had dispatched Tiger Woods in a playoff.

Payne Stewart's religious metamorphosis led him to wear a bracelet with the initials WWJD, What Would Jesus Do. After his death, many players began wearing such bracelets in his honor. Tom Lehman wears a Day-Glo green friendship bracelet, given to him by his daughter.

Mark Wiebe carries quarters. He won't mark his ball on the green with anything else. Seve Ballesteros always brings a change of clothing in bluish hues. Blue is his favorite color, he said, and the color best suited for the final round. "Gray," he said, "is a sad color. Red is too aggressive. You need to be in between for this game. Blue is right." Tell it to Tiger Woods, whose color of choice for the final round is red, his power color, according to his mother.

Ballesteros, incidentally, will *not* carry any balls with the number 3 on them. "I don't like them," he said, noting that 3 is the number of putts a player wishes to avoid.

One player refused to carry balls with high numbers on them, claiming that a higher number required more ink, increasing their weight, and costing him distance. Honest.

8

A TOUGH DAY AT THE OFFICE

Anything's possible, according to an old PGA Tour slogan. Indeed, you can never be certain of what you might see in the course of a tournament round, including anything from aces to eighteens and the temper tantrums that the shots that produce the latter kinds of scores tend to engender.

The fact that John Daly is capable of delivering on every count makes him a focal point of any tournament in which he plays. A pairing with Daly guarantees a wild ride, particularly when, in the vernacular of the PGA Tour pro, he begins leaking oil. At the Bay Hill Invitational in 1998, he made an 18 on the sixth hole. He had two hundred seventy yards to carry the water with his second shot and attempted to do so with a 3-wood. The ball came up short, landing in the pond. He took a drop and hit another into the water. And another and another, seven balls all together splashing down before one finally reached the green.

"I was determined to get it over the water," he said. "I had two-seventy to carry, and I was trying to hit that 3-wood over it. The bad thing about it was it was so close to getting over it, every single time. It made me even more mad. But after all was said and done it was pretty funny. It was *Tin Cup* is what it was. Everybody was seeing *Tin Cup*. When I finally got on the green I'm thirty feet and putting for a seventeen and Tom Watson goes, 'John, knock it in.' He was serious. We just started laughing. It's funny. After I got done, Tom said, 'You know, I've done it before; we've all done it. But I would have bailed out a little quicker than you did.'"

Daly was abstaining from alcohol at the time, which might have prevented a worse scene. "There probably would have been a few clubs in the water," he said when asked what might have happened had this occurred during a time he was drinking heavily. "I don't know. It would have been a bigger scene, probably. I would have tried to knock it *in* the water, probably. But I was trying my heart out to knock it over the water."

Incidentally, Daly made a birdie 2 on the next hole, which meant that he played the two holes in 18–2. Or, as he put it, facetiously attempting to paint it in less vivid colors, "it looks like I made a 10 and a 10."

Daly once encountered problems circumnavigating the five-hundred-forty-two-yard fifteenth hole at English Turn in New Orleans, taking a dozen strokes to complete it. The fifteenth is virtually a water hazard from tee to its island green. Daly hit his tee shot into the water, took a drop, then hit his third shot into the rough. When he attempted to reach the island green with his fourth shot using a 2-iron, it came up short and splashed in the water. He hit two more 2-irons into the water and finally reached land on his tenth shot, fortunately, given that his supply of golf balls had dwindled to two. "Today was just a test of patience," he said. Ironically, Daly was on record as saying that his goal that year was to focus on every shot.

At the Memorial in 1999, he took six putts on the eighteenth hole, a demonstration of impatience that led to the suspicion that he might have resumed drinking. "No, I'm not drinking," he said. "I'm just playing bad golf." Daly had reached the green in four, leaving him with an eight-footer for bogey. He ran that one eight feet past the hole, then started slapping the ball at the hole, eventually navigating the final four feet in three putts. "The sad part," he said, "is I tried on four of them."

When Daly opened the U.S. Open at Pinehurst with a 68, he praised the setup, particularly the crowned greens and the closely mowed fringes that failed to slow a ball's progress, permitting it to roll off the green, to a collection area.

"I do think the greens are similar to St. Andrews, the way the USGA shaved them down," he said. By Sunday, he had changed his mind. On one hole, Daly attempted to putt the ball up the slope and onto the green, but he failed to rap it hard enough and it began rolling back toward him. His supply of patience having expired, Daly began walking up the slope and took a swipe at his rolling ball, in the manner of a polo player, sending it careening across the green. He was assessed a two-stroke penalty for hitting a moving ball.

Afterward, Daly declared that he would never play another U.S. Open, a threat he recanted the following day when his benefactors at Callaway Golf sternly suggested he apologize to the USGA.

At the Scandinavian Masters one year, Daly tossed his driver into a lake. "I wasn't mad," he explained. "I just didn't ever want to see it again."

En route to a third-round 77 that eliminated him from contention at the PGA Championship at Winged Foot in 1997, Daly hit a drive straight right on the twelfth hole, a shot for which his driver was found guilty by Judge Daly, who sentenced it to expulsion. He flung it over a fence. "It wasn't a throw," Daly explained, "it was a just a toss, really. A throw is when you throw it as hard as you can." The club was retrieved and returned to Daly at the next hole, but its sentence was not commuted. He declined to use it the rest of the round.

Daly's horrific shots typically are those that are navigationally challenged, similar to a plane that travels a long distance and lands at the wrong airport, miles off course. Yet some of the worst shots in professional golf are the shortest ones. Michael Bradley was leading the Doral-Ryder Open when he lipped out a birdie putt on the eleventh hole of the final round, leaving him a ten-inch tap-in for par. He went through his routine, pulled the putter back, and stroked the gimme putt, only to see it turn left, catching the lip, and spinning out. "I can't explain it," he said later. "I still don't really know what happened."

Bradley at least regrouped and went on to win the tournament. Hale Irwin missed a shorter putt once, and it cost him the British Open. He had a tap-in putt of no more than a few inches and somehow whiffed it. He had gotten careless and sort of waved his putter at it and missed. He eventually tied for second, a stroke behind the winner, Tom Watson.

When Lanny Wadkins missed a putt he thought he should have made (most of those he missed, incidentally, were in this category), he often indifferently backhanded the next one. He tried this at the ninth hole at Augusta National in 1991, after missing a four-footer. The one-footer spun out of the hole, resulting in a double bogey. Wadkins eventually lost the tournament by two strokes.

Davis Love III once took a practice stroke with his putter but discovered too late that he was standing too close to his ball, inadvertently hitting it. What he should have done at that point was replace the ball and assess himself a one-stroke penalty. Instead he assumed that the inadvertent stroke counted and that he was required to play his next shot from where the ball had stopped. Wrong. The penalty for failing to return the ball to its original position was two strokes. When Love signed for a 4 instead of a 5, he was disqualified. The mistake cost him $105,437, the money he'd have earned had he not been disqualified.

Paul Azinger probably wishes he could have been DQ'd the day he missed a tap-in putt, the ball spinning out and hitting his shoe, resulting in a two-stroke penalty. All told he needed four strokes to hole out from a matter of inches.

Players occasionally are forced to withdraw for any variety of reasons, usually injury-related. David Feherty once withdrew with a strained back after playing two holes on a Saturday morning. His drive at the second hole convinced him his day was over. "It didn't suffer," he said of the drive, "because it was dead before it hit the ground."

He was asked about his day afterward. "I shot twelve," he said. "I'm bound to be leading."

Sometimes a player will exit the course for reasons other than injury. Nature does not extend a pass to the professional tournament golfer, even as he is on display to throngs in the gallery and at home watching on television. So, then, when nature calls, how do players answer?

Richard Edmondson of the British broadsheet *The Independent* addressed the situation while covering the British Open at Royal Birkdale, when an American, Steve Stricker, heeded the call.

"When you do this sort of thing on a municipal it is usually easy to find a quiet thicket," Edmondson wrote. "It is not quite the same at the Open amid 40,000 people. Stricker set off into the coastal jungle and gradually his cap disappeared from view. There were sand-lizards and other beasties in the direction he was heading. Bold Steve scythed a path out some time later and rejoined us on the fairway. 'Much needed,' the American said. Then he got a birdie."

A visit to the loo does not ensure a birdie, of course. The game is not that simple, as players routinely lament. At the Players Championship in 1999, Bob Friend made the cut, but shot an 87 in the third round. He was first off on Sunday. Since an odd number of players had made the cut, he was required to play alone, in front of a small, but friendly crowd. "I think everybody felt sorry for me," he said. "Here's a guy playing by himself after shooting a snowman with a hockey stick [87]."

In the same tournament, Steve Stricker was in contention when he began to stumble, hitting pine needles, a spectator, and a sand trap in one particular two-hole stretch. "The wheels just fell off," he said, using a phrase that ordinarily is the exclusive domain of the amateur. "No matter what I tried to do I couldn't keep myself from hitting it sideways. I was just trying to survive and not beat myself up coming in."

Tempers fray in professional golf, to the same degree as or more intensely than they do every Saturday morning on the local municipal course.

"I love throwing clubs," said Steve Pate, whose nickname is "Volcano." "It's just not acceptable. I've had fifteen years to regret some of the things I've done."

A reporter asked him to single out the worst of them.

"I have to pick just one?" he asked.

Pate wrapped a club around a tree once, snapping the shaft, though his young daughter Nicole was concerned only with the condition of the tree.

"Why'd you hurt it, Daddy?" she asked.

"Because it got in the way," Pate replied. "Shouldn't have been there."

CBS commentator Gary McCord kindly offered to cover for him in the event of an eruption, by talking over him, so that the boom mike would not relay a string of expletives over the airways.

The man who set the standard for eruptions was Tommy Bolt, who, so the story goes, once came to a long par-3 and asked his caddie what club was required.

"A 6-iron," the caddy replied.

A 6-iron wasn't enough club, Bolt knew. Why, he asked, do you recommend the 6-iron?

"That's the only club you have left in the bag," the caddy replied, "other than the putter and it sure isn't a putt."

Bolt offered advice for the club throwers: "Always throw them ahead of you, so you don't have to waste energy going back to pick them up." He also said, "I probably held distance records for every club in the bag." The PGA eventually put in place what was dubbed the "Tommy Rule," which prohibited the throwing of clubs. Bolt adamantly wanted to be the first to violate it; the day after the rule went into effect, he tossed his putter, an infraction for which he was fined.

It is better to break a club than a bone, of course. Mark Calcavecchia kicked a camera tower once, breaking a toe. "Very, very stupid," he said. He too has been susceptible to eruption, though at the outset of a new year he resolved to control his temper. He was tested at the Doral Ryder Open when he made a 10 on the par-5 tenth hole. "It was a good 10," he said, demonstrating his control. "I got a sand save out of it."

Ben Crenshaw's nickname was Gentle Ben, which reflected his gentle demeanor off the course. He is among the most gracious men in the history of golf. On the course, however, he often exhibited a short fuse. Once he was exasperated by missing a putt and tossed his putter in the air. His attempt at catching it failed, and the head of the putter hit him in the head, opening a bloody wound.

Tiger Woods has been known to break ground with the business end of a club that has failed to deliver the requisite result. He did so after hooking a drive into the left rough in a quarterfinal loss to Jeff Maggert at the WGC Andersen Consulting Match Play Championship. In fact, his frequent televised tantrums led some to conclude that he was not having a great deal of fun. Early in 1999, his father Earl borrowed from Walter Hagen and advised Tiger "to stop and smell the roses."

"I think that frown all the time, and that slamming the club down, doesn't do anything for his game and the game of golf," Arnold Palmer said in a pointed interview in March of 1999. "He's got the world in his hands. All he has to do is enjoy it and laugh, and enjoy the ability he has to the fullest extent. He's not convincing anybody of anything when he slams a club down. They know he's good. He's already proved that."

The inherent problem is that golf is a malicious game that inevitably tests the limits of a player's temper. When the game pushes too hard, an eruption occurs, outwardly for some. For others, "it burns inwardly and scars the soul," Bobby Jones wrote.

Even with the world watching, some cannot contain their emotions, and it does not leave a favorable impression. "I can't believe the actions of some of our top pros," Fuzzy Zoeller once said. "They should have second jobs modeling for Pampers."

Fred Couples's anger manifests itself in a way that is more in line with his easygoing demeanor. When he walks down a fairway twirling his club between his fingers, in the manner of a baton, he probably is angry with himself.

Couples once was on the receiving end of Greg Norman's anger, though it was not intentionally directed toward him. Norman tossed a ball in anger, but his direction was skewed and the ball struck Couples in the chest.

Larry Silveira's temper once took its toll on him off the course. He was in La Jolla for the Buick Invitational in 1997. While attempting to do a load of laundry, he became angry when the machine declined to accept his quarters. He punched out the machine, breaking his hand in the process, then learned that the machine would not accept his quarters because it had been transformed into a free machine.

Ken Green must be among the tour's all-time leaders in fines, as well as the diverse ways he earns them. He was fined once for drinking a beer during a Masters round. Obscene language at the AT&T Pebble Beach National Pro-Am as well as a tirade directed at Raymond Floyd at the Masters earned him a ninety-day suspension and a $3,500 fine,

John Daly is renowned for his lack of patience. At the World Series of Golf in 1994, Daly and the father of another competitor engaged in an impromptu wrestling match in the parking lot, both of them tumbling to the pavement before bystanders separated them.

Daly had shot an 83 that day and apparently had driven into the

group ahead of him on two successive holes. PGA club pro champion Jeffrey Roth was a part of that group, and one of the shots, he
said, flew past at a pretty good clip. Angry words were exchanged
afterward.

En route to the parking lot, Daly and Roth's father, Bob,
exchanged words, according to witnesses. Roth then grabbed Daly
by the shoulder, and round one was under way. It ended quickly,
and the upshot was that Daly left the tour "on voluntary leave," a
euphemism for suspension, for the next three-plus months.

Periodically, others threaten to transform golf from the quiet
gentility that ordinarily defines it into a contact sport. One of the
more infamous disagreements occurred between Greg Norman
and Mark McCumber. The former accused the latter of cheating
at the World Series one year, by using his thumb to tamp down a
spike mark on his putting line. McCumber acknowledged touch-
ing a spike mark, but only when he was brushing away an insect.

Norman was so angry that he threatened to withdraw, though
his wife and PGA Tour commissioner Tim Finchem intervened.
Three days later Norman holed a sixty-six-foot chip shot in a
sudden-death playoff to win the tournament.

Mark Wiebe and Fred Funk nearly came to blows after the bell
had rung, ending round three, to borrow from boxing. The disagreement began on the eighteenth hole at the MasterCard
Colonial, where we let Funk pick up the action. "With Wiebe,
everything disturbs him," Funk said. "Sharon [Funk's wife and
caddy that week] and I were conscious of it, and we stayed out of
his way. On eighteen, I think he thought I was ready to putt, but it
was clearly his play. So I told him, 'Wiebs, I think you're out.' And
he told me to '. . . get out of my way.'"

Near the scoring tent, Funk and Wiebe's caddy Terry Travis
began arguing, triggering a profane exchange between Funk and
Wiebe that carried over into the clubhouse. "I don't know what it
is," Wiebe said, "whether he thinks he should be ranked higher,

making more money, or winning more. It just seems like something else is eating him."

Funk later was reprimanded by the tour for conduct unbecoming a professional.

"I got berated by someone who should have been in a straitjacket," Wiebe told the *Dallas Morning News*. "He went through a total meltdown, right in front of everybody. I've never been that embarrassed for anybody in my life."

Funk apologized to all involved, save for Wiebe, whose "whole tone and attitude is so offensive," Funk said, "that I just lost complete control of my emotions."

Their relationship is so contentious that the future is predictable: a mischievous organization—either the USGA or the PGA of America—succumbing to the temptation to bring them together in a rematch by intentionally pairing them at some point in the future.

Daly's appeal is his length as well as the fact that he does not fit the PGA Tour stereotype. The crowds he tends to attract, like many of those swept into the game by the tidal wave of Tigermania, aren't necessarily savvy in the etiquette of the game. Give these fans an ample supply of beer and a hot sun, and you have a potential for misbehavior.

The sixteenth hole at the Phoenix Open has become a magnet for those who overindulge in the heat and become somewhat more vocal than the typical golf crowd. Phoenix attracts such huge crowds that they are routinely disruptive, particularly when they are rooting for someone. One such time, Phil Mickelson, a product of Arizona State University and a resident of Scottsdale, was contending with Justin Leonard for the Phoenix Open title. The crowd openly rooted for Mickelson and against Leonard, shouting at him to miss putts and cheering when he obliged them.

"There were one hundred fifty thousand people cheering for the guy I was playing against, there was alcohol served, and the Super Bowl was there [in Tempe, Arizona] the next day," Leonard said. "You can imagine some of the things that were said. Only the people there at the tournament, walking, know how tough that really was."

It was tough enough that he ultimately lost to Mickelson on the third hole of a sudden-death playoff. "They were obnoxious out there in Phoenix and it got to him," Leonard's caddy Bob Riefke said.

Still, Leonard has returned, year after year. He concluded that three or four unruly spectators in a crowd of more than a hundred thousand were not sufficient to keep him from coming back. "I really learned a lot that week," he said, "and it's something that I still carry with me. Hey, I want to win tournaments, but sometimes you learn a little more from losses like that. I think that tournament made me a better golfer, by going out and playing well in some adversity. It wasn't a negative experience at all."

By 1999, Leonard was in contention again at Phoenix, this time attempting to overtake Rocco Mediate. This time the crowd was rooting for him, even at the sixteenth hole. So, he was asked, you've converted them?

"Well, you know, they're so foggy," he said, "they probably don't remember I was here three years ago that late in the day."

John Cook is among those who elect to pass on the Phoenix Open, which he called a circus. Some don't go to the Greater Greensboro Open for much the same reasons.

The later in the day—as the beer begins to take its toll—the greater the potential for hostility, as Greg Norman learned the week after his Masters collapse in 1996. He was playing in the MCI Classic, and as he left the eighteenth tee, a man yelled at him, "Why did you choke last week? You cost me money."

Norman's caddy, Tony Navarro, intervened on his behalf, grabbing the heckler and pushing him, causing him to tumble to the ground.

"That's assault and battery," the fan yelled. "I'm going to sue Greg Norman."

The heckler then turned to a marshal, according to eyewitness accounts, and asked, "You saw that, didn't you?"

"All I saw," the marshal reportedly said, "was a drunk redneck being obnoxious to a golfer."

Norman's playing partner that day was Charlie Rymer, a South Carolina native, who apologized to Norman on behalf of the entire state. "That's a real shame," Rymer said. "That's sad to see."

A year later, Norman was playing in the Kemper Open and heard a fan yell, "Chunk it in the water!" Norman was said to have made an obscene gesture in return. Confusion, meanwhile, reigned on all sides. The fan claimed to have yelled to the man known as the Shark, "Chum is in the water!" Norman said he did not respond with an obscene gesture, that he considered doing so, but simply "went up with the fist" instead. Tom Lehman was playing with Norman that day, and he too thought he heard the fan imploring Norman to "chunk it in the water!" The man, however, sought out Lehman after the round to explain what he had said, and Lehman was satisfied that the man indeed had said "chum."

Curtis Strange was on the receiving end of abuse by fans several months after closing his Ryder Cup singles match with three consecutive bogeys, resulting in a key loss to Europe's Nick Faldo in 1995.

"Bogey, bogey, bogey," a spectator yelled at him during the second round of the Honda Classic. "Ryder Cup choker."

Ironically, Strange was paired that day with Faldo, and Faldo identified the man to tournament marshals, who escorted him from the premises. Strange, meanwhile, had to be restrained by another playing partner, Jim Gallagher Jr.

"At the time, I wanted to confront the guy," Strange said. "It certainly crossed my mind. But then you get down to his level. That's not the way to go about it."

For Scott Hoch, a cumbersome cross to bear has been the fact that he once missed a two-and-a-half-foot putt which would have won him the Masters and that he is frequently reminded that his last name rhymes with "choke." Unable to produce a victory at the Canon Greater Hartford Open in 1998, Hoch was standing by the practice green, the subject of an informal interview session with a few reporters, when a spectator walked by and shouted, "Scott Choke. Choke it up."

Hoch went after him and was on the verge of demonstrating his ability to choke by putting his hands around the man's neck for a few seconds before releasing him and walking away.

"The guy said the wrong thing," Hoch said later. "I've heard it several times. I'm just glad I did what I did, because I wanted to hit him."

Golf has a problem unique in sports; the spectators' proximity to the players. Usually only a thin rope separates the fans from the golfers, and when the latter make their way from one green to the next tee they are required to move through the crowd, which typically is parted by volunteer marshals.

"One of our strengths," Phil Mickelson said, "is the interaction that a player can have with fans, how close we are. I also think at times we might be just a little bit too close."

Too close for comfort?

"I've thought about it, and we'd be the easiest athletes to pick off if somebody wanted to," Steve Stricker told the *Columbus Dispatch*. "If somebody wanted to get you, there's not enough security in the world to stop them."

Security issues came to the fore at the Phoenix Open in 1999, when a spectator was arrested on suspicion of felony assault on a police officer and disorderly conduct. He was found to have a semiautomatic pistol in his fanny pack, although this did not warrant a charge, since the man had an Arizona permit to carry a concealed weapon.

"It's the booze," John Daly said. "People do crazy things when they're drunk. I have."

Tiger Woods called it scary. Woods is a multiethnic star in a game historically dominated by whites and has been a frequent target of death threats. Typically, he has a phalanx of security personnel escorting him. Still, he'd rather not be informed of such incidents until after his round. "I didn't know and I didn't want to know about the gun until after the last hole," he said. "But I never felt threatened."

The man turned out to be a menace only to himself and reportedly was rooting for Woods. Still, the mix of alcohol and weaponry and marshals asking for quiet, please, is volatile; and the PGA Tour, vehemently, would like to avoid it.

"It's kind of idiotic," Mark Calcavecchia said. "We can get a nut case in a crowd of a thousand. I don't know what the answer is."

The crowds at the Phoenix Open are among the largest in golf—an attendance of 422,650 in 1999—and create unsolvable security problems. Jesper Parnevik, for instance, set down his bag adjacent to the putting green at Phoenix and a fan lifted three Callaway woods and walked off. The clubs were recovered. At the same tournament, Steve Flesch had his clubs stolen from his courtesy car. They, too, were recovered.

Overzealous fans are not yet the nuisance that those with cellular phones are. On his way to a victory in the Kemper Open, Rich Beem was distracted by the ring of a cell phone. "What I can't figure out," he said; "I guarantee you that eighty percent of cell phones today have that vibrating mode. Just do that if you have to have the phone. Is it seriously that important on Memorial Day Saturday? I don't think so. There were a bunch of phones on the golf course. There were a few people out there with cell phones four, five different times, that got to be a little annoying. But, you know, I got through them."

A fan was talking on a cell phone a few feet away from the gallery ropes and the green on which Dicky Pride was attempting to earn a living. "Excuse me," he said. "I'm working here. If you need to work, then go to your office."

Justin Leonard had to step away from a shot and admonish a cell-phone user on three occasions at the Doral-Ryder Open. "I don't ask people to not bring their cell phones," Leonard said. "I just ask them to turn 'em off. But how do you police that? You can't go grabbing every cell phone to see if it's on. It's a tough situation."

And a growing problem, one that the PGA Tour has attempted to address. For several years, the tour prohibited cell phones on the premises, but this was a rule it did not enforce; and in any case the rule is no longer in effect.

"At times, people have been blatant about talking on the phone ten feet from a player who is trying to hit off the tee," Jim Furyk said.

The tour pro's work for the day officially ends when he has signed his scorecard following his round, a formality that sometimes goes awry. Nick Faldo won six major championships, none of them as emotional for him as the British Open at Muirfield in 1992. When the dazed Faldo arrived in the scorer's tent, he realized he had failed to keep the score of his playing partner, Steve Pate, as is customary. What, Faldo asked Pate, should I do?

"Put me down for a 65," replied Pate, who had finished fourth, but would have won with a 65.

The mind-set of the superstar does not allow his focus to wander beyond his own game. A man with whom Ben Hogan was playing once aced the twelfth hole at Augusta National, while Hogan made a birdie 2. As they left the green, Hogan told his playing partner that it was the first time he had ever birdied that hole.

Jack Nicklaus was playing with Phil Rodgers in the final round of the British Open at Muirfield in 1966. Nicklaus ultimately won, but when the duo repaired to the scorer's tent, Nicklaus noticed that he had forgotten to keep his playing partner's score.

"My scorecard was just a blank," Rodgers told *Golf Digest.* "He hadn't written down a thing. Effectively, I wasn't even there. He had got himself into a state of oneness with the course and concentrated on winning the Open."

Players occasionally have trouble adding, which manifests itself occasionally in the signing of an incorrect scorecard. This would seem a virtual impossibility, given the simplicity with which a card is reconciled. Each player is responsible for recording the score, hole by hole, of his playing partner and is given an official tournament scorecard for that purpose. Each card also has a perforated attachment with another line on which the player records his own scores. At the end of the round, the player tears off his own score line, which he uses to match up with the hole-by-hole scores recorded by his playing partner. Any discrepancy ought to jump out at him. Inexplicably, this system does not always work to perfection.

The most egregious and costly penalty for signing an incorrect scorecard occurred at the PGA Tour Qualifying Tournament in 1999. This is a player's most stringent test; pass here and you graduate to the PGA Tour. Fail and you are sentenced to another year in the minor leagues. In a grueling six-round affair, the top thirty-five from a field of one hundred sixty-nine earn their PGA Tour playing privileges.

In this qualifying tournament, Jaxon Brigman once missed an eight-foot birdie putt on the eighteenth hole of the final round and dejectedly walked off the course, thinking he had missed earning his card by a single shot. Brigman hastily signed for a round of 65, the number that he had actually shot. Later on, officials added the numbers and the sum was 66. His playing partner had put a 4 where a 3 belonged, and Brigman had failed to notice the error. He signed the card, which gave him a 66, rather than a 65, a stroke of carelessness that proved to be the difference; he had erred in his assessment of what he needed to shoot and missed earning his PGA Tour card by a single shot. When he learned of his mistake, he fell to the ground weeping.

Even established stars occasionally lapse. Payne Stewart, a winner of the U.S. Open and PGA Championship, signed his card after the second round of the Southwestern Bell Colonial in 1994, though no number had been entered in the box for the ninth hole. He was disqualified.

Bernhard Langer and Grant Waite were both disqualified from the same tournament for signing incorrect scorecards. Waite signed for a 4 on the fourteenth hole, where he actually made a 5, while Langer did the same thing on the seventeenth hole.

Paul Azinger once was disqualified, not for signing an incorrect card, but for failing to sign his card at all. He had played with Mac O'Grady, one of the more eccentric players in golf history. O'Grady was keeping Azinger's score and on precisely one-third of the holes, six of eighteen, he wrote down the wrong number. In the scoring tent afterward, Azinger had to unscramble the mess O'Grady had made of his card, and in the confusion he forgot to attach his signature to it.

"You've got to be a total idiot," Tommy Tolles said, speaking about scorecard errors in general and confessing on behalf of an entire industry, "and sometimes we are."

9

MEET THE PRESS

Armed robbery obviously is not a laughing matter, unless it is introduced in the press tent, where gallows humor vies with sarcasm and cynicism for equal time.

Payne Stewart was in the press room once recounting a harrowing tale that unfolded en route from one tour stop to another. He was asleep in the backseat of a van driven by a friend, Jim Morris, who had his wife along. They stopped at a fast-food restaurant, and Morris went to the men's room. When Morris came out, he encountered a robber holding a gun to his wife's head.

"I can't imagine that," Stewart said, "to walk around the corner and see somebody with a gun to your wife's head."

"Where," whispered one reporter entangled in contentious divorce proceedings, "can I find a guy like that?"

So it goes in the press room, where nothing is sacred, least of all a solemn occasion or harrowing tale. The press room is a battleground of sorts, a place where a game of reverence encounters irreverence, where reporters attempt to pry colorful quotes from players who seemingly are steadfast in their resolve not to relinquish one. Occasionally the questions are dumb and the answers are dumber. To wit, or dimwit, in the case of the interrogator in the following exchange:

"There's a kind of perception out there," the man asked David Duval, "that you're somewhat of a dullard."

"A what?" Duval said, uncertain that he was hearing the question correctly.

"A dullard. Why do you think that is?"

"You tell me. Is that your impression?"

"I don't know."

"I don't understand. You haven't clarified whether you're talking about my personality or my golf game."

"Personality. I don't mean to be offensive."

Too late.

That was dumb. This was dumber:

In the course of an exchange at the British Open, Mark O'Meara was discussing Ryder Cup compensation and suggested that since the players weren't getting paid and reporters seemed to have no problem with that, perhaps they, too, ought to work gratis that week, donating their salaries to charity.

One reporter countered by noting that writers aren't multimillionaires.

"I'm not either," O'Meara said with no more conviction than a cornered politician denying an office liaison. The 9,000-square-foot lakefront home equipped with an elevator; the two boats—one for fishing, one for skiing—tied to the private dock in the back, in the tony gated community of Isleworth outside Orlando, Florida; the garage full of luxury automobiles; and PGA Tour earnings in excess of $11 million gave him away.

O'Meara quickly backed down from his assertion. Lest this indiscretion leave the wrong impression, O'Meara is among the more engaging players in golf, a gentleman, as he has demonstrated routinely during his twenty-year career, including one particular exchange with a neophyte golf writer. O'Meara was in the interview room adjacent to the press tent and was describing a nasty breeze as a two-club wind.

"Which two clubs?" the reporter asked.

O'Meara to his credit refrained from belittling the reporter and patiently explained that he meant that the wind had been so strong that instead of hitting, say, a 7-iron approach shot, he'd have to hit a 5-iron. Suffice it to say, many professional athletes would have demonstrated no such patience and would have taken perverse pleasure in embarrassing the reporter.

Occasionally reporters deserve belittling. Jeff Sluman, for instance, was given a green light to shred the reporter who once asked him whether he had the type of game that could win a major championship. "I think so," said Sluman, the winner of the PGA Championship in 1988, "since I've already won a major."

A writer won a major once, too, or at least contributed in a small way. Athletes in every sport have come to realize that writers serve only one useful purpose, to motivate them. It has become a cliché, athletes and teams winning a championship to prove their critics wrong. The critics typically wear press badges.

So it was that Jack Nicklaus came to win the Masters in 1986, at the age of forty-six. Four days before the tournament began, Tom McCollister, the respected golf writer for the *Atlanta Journal-Constitution*, wrote, "Nicklaus is gone, done. He just doesn't have the game anymore. It's rusted from lack of use. He's forty-six, and nobody that old wins the Masters."

Nicklaus was sharing a house that week with his friend and business partner, John Montgomery, who taped the story to the refrigerator, where his housemate was certain to see it, over and over again. Nicklaus did, and it angered him.

The final round of the Masters was among the most memorable in history, Nicklaus tapping into his reservoir of talent once more to shoot a 65 and to win one for the ages, or in this case the aged. Afterward, he sought out McCollister and found him writing on deadline.

"Thanks, Tom," Nicklaus said simply.

Ernie Els is an affable sort who nonetheless was taken aback by a question from a local radio reporter following the third round of the PGA Championship at the Riviera Country Club in 1995.

"Considering the way you're playing," she asked, "isn't a three-shot lead insurmountable?"

"Have you been around, lady?" Els replied.

The next day, Els squandered that three-stroke lead and tied for third, Steve Elkington defeating Colin Montgomerie in a playoff.

The writer-player relationship frequently is an adversarial one, and memories are long. Warmth was scarce one day, when a writer noted, "It's colder in the press room than a Vijay Singh interview." Singh's relationship with the media historically is strained.

The estimable Dan Jenkins, in his *Golf Digest* column, once poked fun at professional golfers by offering tips on how they might avoid "media heat." He concluded by sarcastically suggesting statements that might help the golfer end a conversation with a golf writer. Among them: "You're so smart, how much you make, anyhow?"

At least one golfer, O'Meara, has invoked the question. When he was queried as to why his performance had fallen in the wake of a year in which he won the Masters and the British Open, O'Meara countered by noting that he had made more than $600,000 to that point of the year, then asked, "How much have you guys made?"

If money were the barometer by which success is gauged, Colombian drug lords would consider Tiger Woods a failure. Athletes tend to use this barometer to illustrate what they perceive to be the higher station they occupy in life. The interview room reinforces this notion. Set up so that players sit on a platform and peer down on the assembled reporters, the press room creates the perception that the reporters are worshiping at the players' feet.

The ignominious task of having to mingle with the unwashed notwithstanding, an invitation to the press room is among the most coveted in professional golf; it is confirmation of a job well done. Generally, only those in or near the lead after each round are invited to the press tent to participate in a group interview for the benefit of the players, who otherwise would be besieged for a series of one-on-one interviews.

When Tiger Woods and Sergio Garcia dueled to the wire at the PGA Championship and became the talk of the golf world, David Duval seemed to have become irrelevant, a situation with which he was not necessarily happy, despite his reticence about opening up to the media. "I don't want anybody to stop talking to me," Duval said at the Sprint International the following week, "because that means I am not playing well."

Scott Hoch learned this firsthand. He once announced that he was no longer speaking with the media, the culmination of an ongoing feud. After shooting a 65 one day, he attempted to explain his decision. At one point, he was asked whether his vow of silence would continue. "It hasn't been in too much force," he said, "because I found out that nobody wants to talk to you much when you don't do very well."

Still, players often treat a trip to the interview room as though it were a root canal, an appropriate analogy, given the fact that extracting an interesting quotation from them is often akin to pulling teeth. Payne Stewart was often less than accommodating before his spiritual transformation in the last few years of his life provided him with the maturity and amicability that occasionally had been lacking in his demeanor. The media were not alone in bearing the brunt of the man *Golf World* described as an "angry, quick-tempered boor," after he missed the cut at the Masters in 1994 and snapped at anyone crossing his path, including a woman requesting an autograph. Stewart refused to sign and stormed away, leaving his wife, Tracey, to find the woman in the parking lot and apologize on behalf of her husband.

"When my wife has to start apologizing for my behavior," Stewart said, "it's time to admit I have a problem."

He also found perspective in the cancer that had stricken his friend Paul Azinger. The two of them went fishing for a couple of days. "I couldn't help thinking, 'Here's a guy who's going to beat cancer, and I'm worried about my golf game?' That's pretty selfish."

Stewart once took a lead into the final round of the AT&T Pebble Beach National Pro-Am, played poorly, and finished second, much to his dismay. Though the PGA Tour requires that the winner and the runner-up report to the interview room, Stewart went straight from the eighteenth green at Pebble Beach to his car, trailed by a pack of reporters searching for an explanation for his collapse.

"I'll talk to you next week," said Stewart, who was playing in the Hawaiian Open the following week and surely was aware that the horde of reporters on hand weren't making the trek.

"I was gone, my car was in the lot, and I was hot," he said, recalling the incident after winning the AT&T in 1999. "I wasn't mature then. I was immature. I've grown up a lot. I know how important it is what you all do for a living. I'm a lot older and I'm a lot wiser, too. I'm more mature. I grew so much last year at the U.S. Open. I grew in how I deal with all of you. I was actually pleasant, wasn't I?"

In his first year as a professional, Tiger Woods failed to grasp why he was targeted by an insatiable press corps, why he alone was required to agree to a group interview week in and week out, even day in and day out. The Nike contract, which was paying him on average $8 million annually, ought to have been a sufficient hint. If interest in Woods had not been so substantial, neither would the Nike contract.

Two months after winning the Masters by twelve shots, Woods, twenty-one, played poorly in the first round of the U.S. Open and declined a media interview, even failing to stop in the corral area set up by the United States Golf Association to give reporters an opportunity to talk with players as they come off the course.

A pool reporter eventually trailed him to his car and coerced a few innocuous quotes from him before he angrily flung a portable CD player into the car, slammed the door, and sped away. The following day, he shot 67 and again was invited to the interview room. This time he agreed and was queried about his snub of the press the day before.

QUESTION: Tiger, can you explain why you chose not to talk to the media, whether it was just your frustration from the double (bogey), or what was it yesterday?

WOODS: Why would you want to talk to a guy who is nine shots back? I think there may be a double standard. Do you require Greg Norman or Steve Elkington or Phil Mickelson, who ended up at five-over, to come in? They don't require that. And I have to come in? I just want to be considered one of the one hundred fifty-six players playing the tournament. And if I'm not near the lead, then I shouldn't be required to answer questions. If I am, then great, I will, because I'm near the lead. You're supposed to be asked questions. But when I'm that far back I see no need.

QUESTION: We talked to all sorts of people who are four or five shots or nine shots behind if they're big names. For example, Greg Norman shot a 75 yesterday. He was quite gracious. People are interested in you, and even when you don't play well, they would like to know why. Can you explain why you don't want to even stop and talk to us when we're all assembled out here?

WOODS: What happens is I have to do that every week. And, you know, there's going to be times when I'm not going to play well, and there are times when any guy who's big, whether it's

Norman or Ernie Els, or whoever . . . they don't play well, they
don't have to talk to the media because they're not playing well
and they're not anywhere near the lead. . . . So, hence, I feel
that it is a right for me to decline if I'm that far out of it. I was
nine shots back. I was way out of it. And today I shot myself
back into it. So then I feel I'm obligated to come in here
because I am back in the tournament.

The trade-off for those who acquire fame and fortune is obligation. Nike, Titleist, Rolex, Wheaties, et al. have not been enrich-
ing them to maintain a low profile. Over time, Woods came to
understand his role and has become as accommodating as possible for one with so many demands on his time. His maturity was
apparent in the aftermath of his victory in the Buick Invitational
in La Jolla, California, in early 1999. After the awards celebration,
he was asked to make an appearance at the Century Club
Pavilion. Rather than wince, Woods replied, "That's where all the
rich people are, right?"

"Would you like me to carry the trophy for you?" asked Rick
Schloss, the publicity director for the tournament.

"No," Woods replied. "I worked too hard all week for it. I want
to carry it."

Woods initially was condescending in interviews. "You guys don't
understand," he said, reciting this phrase *ad nauseam*. Eventually he
came to understand that dealing with the media is a necessary evil,
that he needn't automatically consider the press the enemy. Now,
unfailingly, he looks his inquisitors in the eye and answers their questions without rancor, even when they veer off line in the manner of
a misdirected putt, as one notable question did.

"When you have a cold," someone asked Woods, "do you have
chicken soup?"

The contentious interview, a sporting mainstay in odorous stadium and arena locker rooms, is rare in golf, but occasionally

unavoidable. At the U.S. Open at Pinehurst, Woods was asked about comments his father Earl had made disparaging Scotland in an article in *Icon* magazine. "That's for white people," Earl had said of Scotland. "It sucks as far as I'm concerned. It has the sorriest weather. People had better be happy that the Scots lived there instead of the soul brothers. The game of golf would have never been invented. . . . We wouldn't have been stupid enough to go out in that weather and play a silly-ass game and freeze to death. We would have been inside listening to jazz, laughing and joking and drinking rum."

Tiger, in a voice void of resentment, invoked the "deny, deny, deny" defense favored by a man caught cheating on his wife. The conversation:

"Tiger, I'm sure you're aware of your dad's comments that have been reported—about what he said about Scotland," a reporter asked. "I wanted to give you a chance to talk about it. What do you think about what he said?"

"He didn't say it," Woods replied.

"The reporter says she has it on tape."

"He didn't say it. My dad is not like that. He's definitely not like that. My dad knows that Scotland is a wonderful place. The weather is not what it is in Southern California, that's for sure, and everyone knows that. But my dad didn't mean any harm if he did say it. But I don't think he even said it."

Of course he said it. The conversation indeed was on tape, as most interviews are these days, and other reporters eventually heard Earl Woods's travelogue narrative.

Many reporters now carry tape recorders. For those who don't, many tournaments now provide court reporters to transcribe interviews. This is useful in helping clarify confusion, on those occasions when a player claims that his words were "taken out of *content*," as John Daly once did. He was attempting to defend himself against criticism for suggesting that many tour players use drugs.

Among the tournaments employing court reporters is the British Open, which in 1998 lost something in the translation from English to English. Woods was speaking of the crazy flight patterns of shots struck from the rough, balls fluttering toward greens like knuckleballs. "A Niekro would be proud of the shots you can hit," Woods said referring to baseball's Niekro brothers, Phil and Joe, each of them an accomplished knuckleball pitcher. On the official transcription of the interview, it quoted Woods as saying, "A Negro would be proud of the shots you can hit."

Bill Glasson, a quiet man with a dry wit capable of producing a surprisingly good interview, once became angered at what he had read in an Arizona newspaper and quit talking to the media. It was not immediately apparent to the media, however. In other sports, reporters attempt to speak to the same players on a daily basis and readily know when they are being snubbed. In golf, different reporters are on hand as the tour moves from city to city, and each group is interested in interviewing only the superstars or those in contention. Unless Glasson was in contention and his presence was required in the interview room, who would know about his vow of silence?

Glasson even asked PGA Tour media officials to cover for him, by making excuses for his absence on those occasions when his presence was requested. One tour official never got the message and was chastised by Glasson for blowing his cover.

Players generally don't show up in the press room uninvited, though a newspaper article might compel them to drop in to deliver an angry rebuttal. The media room at the Nissan Open is located in the cold, dank, dirty cart barn adjacent to the first fairway at the Riviera Country Club in Pacific Palisades, California. One year, Jerry Kelly was disturbed by what Thomas Bonk had written about him in the *Los Angeles Times* that morning. After hitting his drive from the elevated tee box on the first hole, Kelly made his way down the hill, then suddenly veered left and into the media room in search of Bonk. In *mid-hole*. A sports psychologist isn't required to note Kelly's lack of focus on the job at hand.

Art Spander, a venerable American writer freelancing for a Scottish publication at the British Open in 1999, wrote a column to which David Duval took exception. Duval went in search of Spander, found him in the press tent and delivered a stern rebuke. So did Sam Torrance's wife, after Spander wrote a cheeky, off-beat column, according to his editor's wishes.

The press room (usually a tent) is a catchall for players, who find many uses for it other than the one for which it was intended. El Niño was wreaking havoc on the West Coast in the winter of 1998, when the phone rang in the press room at the Buick Invitational a few days before the start of the tournament.

"This is Fred Couples," the voice on the other end said. "I'm in Los Angeles. What's the weather going to be like tomorrow? I'm trying to decide whether to drive down tonight so I can play a practice round or just wait until tomorrow."

"Let me look outside," said Rick Schloss, director of public relations for the tournament, who was bewildered that he was being pressed into service as an amateur meteorologist. "Looks good right now, but I can't control the rain. It's your call. I'd come down tonight. At least you're here."

"Yeah, maybe I'll do that," Couples replied.

Tournament press rooms frequently receive phone calls Sunday afternoon from those inquiring how much money a certain player made. Eventually, one press room official reached the conclusion that players were calling without identifying themselves and wanted to know how much to pay their caddies, who unlike their employers often live from paycheck to paycheck.

Journalists are capable of earning their reputation, which among the bottom-feeders of professions is perhaps unrivaled. Steve Pate won the Tournament of Champions leading wire to wire in 1988, which meant that he was invited to the press room each day. For the daily newspaper writers, creating a fresh angle on the same player day in and day out is a cumbersome undertaking. They prefer a different leader providing a fresh angle at the end of each day.

A week later, a writer was talking with Dan Forsman, who had taken the first-round lead in the Bob Hope Chrysler Classic, and explained how refreshing it was to have a new face in the interview room, that the week before it was a daily dose of Pate. The writer unwittingly was informing Forsman that his presence would not be particularly welcome in the days ahead.

When Tiger Woods returned to Augusta National a year after winning the Masters, he was selecting the menu for the champions dinner and chose cheeseburgers, perpetually part of his own eat-to-win diet. Craig Stadler, who no doubt had consumed his share of cheeseburgers over time, was asked whether he planned on ordering one that night. "Don't you have anything better to ask?" he replied.

Sometimes no.

Justin Leonard missed a two-foot putt at the PGA Championship one year, eliciting this question: "How can you miss a two-foot putt?" His response: "Have you ever misspelled a word?"

Brian Henninger once qualified for the Masters by winning the Deposit Guaranty Golf Classic when the event had two of its four rounds canceled by inclement weather. "So," a reporter asked Henninger, "how do you feel about skanking your way into the Masters?"

Wayne Westner double-hit a chip shot from deep rough by the seventeenth hole during the third round of the U.S. Open at Oakland Hills. The always helpful media were there to remind him that T.C. Chen suffered a similar fate at the Open at Oakland Hills in 1985. "I'm not particularly interested," Westner replied.

Occasionally an interloper joins the mainstream golf press and unwittingly announces his presence with his first question. David Duval was the target of such a query at the Franklin Templeton Shark Shootout in November of 1999. The Shark Shootout is an end-of-year event hosted by Greg Norman for the purpose of raising significant amounts of money for charity. It is a two-man team event and is as low-key as professional tournament golf gets. It matters neither who wins nor who loses, and the only real objective for the players is to have fun.

At this event, a writer representing *Millionaire* magazine, which in this demographic group perhaps put him more in the mainstream than the traditional golf writer, asked Duval: "David, what is it in your background or developmental makeup that gives you the ability to such an extent that you can focus with such intensity on the course?"

"I've got to psychoanalyze myself *here?*" Duval replied.

At the AT&T Pebble Beach National Pro-Am in 1994, Johnny Miller was a daily visitor to the interview room, but this time the same face was a welcome one. Miller is an outspoken proponent of honesty, as his role as a commentator on NBC golf telecasts has demonstrated. This in concert with the possibility that he might win the event made for a compelling story each day. By this point of his career, Miller played only one or two tournaments a year, which would render a victory in this event as improbable as any in golf history.

His amateur partner that week was Bryant Gumbel, who one day hit a shot that struck a seagull in midflight, sending it plunging to its death. Afterward, Miller was in the interview room fielding a series of related questions and waxing eloquent to an enthralled audience about what a victory would mean to him. In the midst of this exceptional interview, a freelance writer from Britain chimed in with a question that stopped Miller's momentum in its tracks.

"Johnny, have you ever seen anything killed on a golf course before?"

The writer, incidentally, is the same man heard across the press room at the Mercedes Championship at La Costa one year dictating his lead to an editor in Britain: "John Daly comma . . . whose foolishness and stupidity have cost him millions comma . . . "

Foolishness and stupidity are not the exclusive domain of the print media by any stretch. The electronic media tap into reservoirs of each on occasion, too. A radio reporter once spotted Spanish star Seve Ballesteros on the putting green at Augusta National and attempted to get his attention.

"Steve! Steve!" the man shouted at Seve, who paid him no heed.

"Steve! Steve!" the reporter continued, apparently having concluded that his first name was a typographical error, that "Seve" in fact was meant to be "Steve." His persistence eventually angered Seve enough to respond.

"My name is not Steve," Ballesteros said. "My name is Seve. And your name is asshole."

Taiwan's T. C. Chen unexpectedly won the Los Angeles Open in 1987, defeating Ben Crenshaw in a playoff. Chen had virtually no command of English, ensuring a difficult post-tournament news conference. One radio reporter with a reputation for dominating and killing interviews by asking nonsensical questions was undeterred by Chen's lack of command of the English language.

"T.C.," he bellowed from the back of the room, "there are a billion Chinese, and you're here winning this tournament."

A thoroughly confused Chen was speechless and in dire need of an interpreter. Then again, an interpreter was required to translate the question to the rest of the media gathered there as well.

An amusing place, the press tent.

The media, contrary to popular opinion, are capable of demonstrating wit, as PGA Tour commissioner Tim Finchem discovered at the Tour Championship at the Olympic Club in Daly City,

California, one year. Finchem was staging a news conference to announce that Michelob and Mercedes-Benz had come aboard as presenting sponsors of the Tour Championship. Following his remarks, he opened the news conference up to questions.

Up went a hand from the audience of reporters. "Was there any concern when you were making this deal," asked Robinson Holloway, working for Reuters that week, "that your two sponsors represent drinking and driving?"

Finchem, an attorney by trade and accordingly seldom at a loss for words, this time had trouble getting them out. He recovered capably, however, noting that both companies have been responsible in promoting the message that the two activities are incompatible. Meanwhile, representatives of the two companies monitoring the news conference from the back of the room were aghast.

The issue passed and Finchem began fielding other questions. A few moments later, Finchem interrupted another question to revisit Holloway's query, which only served to reignite the issue. "I'd like to go back to Robinson's question," he said. "It's not as bad as some European events that have hard liquor companies as sponsors."

The media abhor a boring quotation and embrace colorful or controversial remarks, these among them:

- "Did anyone tell him he didn't qualify?" Lee Trevino asked in response to Earl Woods's threat to boycott the 1997 Ryder Cup in Spain, because he would not have inside-the-ropes access.
- "He's a little man trying to be a big man," Seve Ballesteros said when asked his opinion of the former PGA Tour commissioner Deane Beman.

The paradox is that the controversial quote the media relish often is used against the man responsible. We ask for honesty from our athletes, then use it to pummel them. Such was the case with Mark Calcavecchia, another strong interview, refreshingly honest and without an internal editor softening the tone of his words. Calcavecchia was playing behind Arnold Palmer in the first round of the Masters in 1999 and was frustrated by his own play. As players leave the Augusta National course, they make their way through a corral adjacent to the clubhouse, a roped-off area that permits the media to mix with the players. Typically, a swarm of reporters are there to talk to each player, as was the case that day. A frustrated Calcavecchia suggested that it's time that Palmer "surrender. He still loves to play golf, but there's no point being out here if you shoot 83–84. Eventually you have to end it, don't you? Look, I would love to see him play great. But he'll probably keep playing until he can't walk anymore."

It was an honest appraisal, but given that the target of his arrow was the beloved Palmer, Calcavecchia was vilified by golf fans and the media alike.

Calcavecchia wrote a letter of apology to Palmer and has taken every opportunity to apologize to him publicly. "I was out of line in saying what I said. It's Arnold Palmer we're talking about here, a legend of the game. And I really had no right to say what I said."

Honesty is a diminishing quality in sports. Diplomacy breeds fewer enemies, and so players typically follow that tack. When Tiger Woods won a tournament his first full year on tour, he spoke about how he had played only his C game. It was an honest assessment (and probably the truth), but it generated animosity among those with whom he must play every day. Their interpretation was that Woods had indicated that the other players weren't good enough to beat him on an off day.

The following week Brad Faxon began a post-round interview by directing a shot at Woods. "I didn't have my A game today," Faxon said. "It was a C-minus. I'm flying in my coaches tomorrow."

Woods defended his words. "All I'm doing is telling the truth," he said. "You ask me a question, and I'll tell you straight out."

Paul Goydos was a lone voice coming to Woods's defense. "He may be the most famous guy in the United States right now," he said. "This is not some guy on a hot streak. Tiger can say whatever he wants. If he doesn't think he's got his A game, he's being honest. That's fine."

Woods was stung by the criticism and no longer assesses his play with a letter grade, any one of which, from A to F, might be good enough to win a tournament, it turns out.

John Daly is among the better interviews in golf, principally because he demonstrates honesty to a fault, however misguided it is.

"I think the bottom line—and you can quote me—is that I suck," he said after shooting rounds of 71 and 79 to miss the cut at the Belgacom Open.

Honesty took another form the day Andy Bean shot 63 at the Shearson Lehman Brothers Open, which was awarding a $50,000 Zero Coupon bond for the low round of the day. Bean was in the press room and had assumed he had a lock on the bond, when it was announced that Craig Stadler also had posted a 63.

"So we split it, right?" Bean asked.

No, the money is rolled over to the next day.

"Which one of you geniuses came up with that idea?" Bean said, a bonus on which he already had counted vanishing in an instant.

Bean, incidentally, conceivably could have *lost* money in the process, via a fine for disparaging a sponsor. The PGA Tour warns its players to use care when speaking with the media. The *PGA Tour Player Handbook and Tournament Regulations*, states:

The favorable public reputation of PGA Tour and its tournaments are valuable assets and create tangible benefits for all PGA Tour members. Accordingly, it is an obligation of member-

ship to refrain from comments to the news media that unreasonably attack or disparage tournaments, sponsors, fellow members,
players or PGA Tour.

Note that the media are excluded from the list of those the players should refrain from attacking unreasonably.

When Daly suggested that many golfers used drugs, Curtis
Strange—another player capable of a pointed, honest statement—
suggested that Daly could go back underneath the rock he crawled
out from. Does this constitute an unreasonable attack?

Fred Couples is a low-key, laid-back, friendly sort. His demeanor
was capable of changing when he was in the throes of a bitter
divorce, a time-tested recipe for evoking anger, particularly when a
newspaper account does not agree with him. Such was
the case when a Florida newspaper columnist tackled the subject
one day.

A short time later, Couples encountered the columnist at a tournament and was unable to keep his anger in check. "Hey, nice
article down there," Couples said to the writer. "Really nice. What
a clown."

Couples nonetheless is among the more affable and popular
players in golf. For a press starved for entertainment, Couples has
proved capable, not so much for the manner in which his answers
tend to meander, leaving thoughts hanging, but for his unique way
of disseminating the truth.

"I'm a lot older than I was when I was thirty," he said when he
was thirty-nine and discussing the idea of playing fewer events in
deference to the onset of age. When he was asked to evaluate his
chances at the MCI Classic in 1995, Couples replied, "This week
I'm a dark shot." Or a long horse. Remember, this was the man
who once said he doesn't like to answer the phone because someone might be on the other end. "It's true," said John Horne, a club
pro who roomed with Couples at the University of Houston. "I

think the only person he ever answered the phone for was me. I'd let it ring thirty times because I knew he was there. Eventually he'd pick it up."

In the media room, cheering is forbidden, unless a playoff is looming, in which case it is considered acceptable to root for the player best situated to prevent overtime. Or, as in the case of Colin Montgomerie at the Masters in 1997, anyone who provides a crystallizing quote on deadline.

After the third round, Woods held a nine-stroke lead, a compelling statement that a changing of the guard in the world of golf was in progress. To put Woods's astonishing domination in better perspective, the media searched for an appropriate quote or two, when Montgomerie ventured into the interview room next to the amphitheater-type press room. Since all interviews at Augusta are piped into the press room to aid those working on deadline, Montgomerie's assessment of the tournament to that point resonated through the adjacent room full of writers.

"All I have to say today is one brief comment," Montgomerie said. "There is no chance. We're all human beings here, but there's no chance humanly possible that Tiger is just going to lose this tournament. No way."

Why would you think that?

"Have you just come in, or have you been away? Have you been on holiday and just arrived?"

It was noted that only a year before Greg Norman had blown a six-stroke lead on Sunday and lost to Nick Faldo by five.

"This is very different," Montgomerie said. "Nick Faldo's not lying second. And Greg Norman's not Tiger Woods."

At that point, a cheer erupted in the press room, dozens of writers on deadline celebrating this defining quote that landed in their laps, or more precisely their laptops.

A playoff was looming as the final round of the U.S. Open at

Pinehurst began winding down. It was becoming increasingly apparent that everyone—a weary press corps included—would have to return on Monday for an eighteen-hole playoff between Payne Stewart and Phil Mickelson. The better story clearly was a victory by Mickelson, whose pregnant wife was home in Arizona, hoping the tournament would end before her labor began. This was a compelling angle that made for an easier story to write.

When Stewart holed the winning putt to avert a playoff, a loud roar reverberated through the press tent, ignited not from any devotion to Stewart, but from the fact that an eighteen-hole playoff the following day had been avoided. The writers were free to go home, which universally and unwaveringly is their only thing they are really rooting for.

Cheering is also permitted when a looming story involves an uninteresting subject or a dull interview promises to be a difficult one to write and the alternative promises to be more compelling, as Dan Jenkins reminded us in *Golf Digest*. "Unless you were a writer on deadline facing the possibility of Marty Furgol winning a tournament," Jenkins wrote, "you didn't know the true meaning of fear."

Jackson Stephens, the former chairman of the Masters, permitted himself to be interviewed each year. He measured his words carefully and delivered them in a painstakingly slow Southern drawl, a combination that was almost sleep-inducing. Listening carefully, however, a reporter might uncover a gem.

Stephens was renowned for stubbornly refusing to permit all eighteen holes of a Masters round to be televised, invoking the heritage of the Augusta National's icons Bobby Jones and Clifford Roberts, who thought only the back nine should be telecast. It was an annual rite, the media quizzing Stephens on this subject. Finally, a writer wondered aloud what would happen if the National Football League ever elected only to air the second half of the Super Bowl.

"Mr. Stephens," the reporter asked, "do you ever watch the Super Bowl?"

Stephens leaned toward the microphone.

"Fourth quarter," he said.

Another time, Stephens was asked whether the Augusta National might become a no-smoking course as others around the country had.

Stephens said nothing. He merely slid a pack of cigarettes from his shirt pocket, then returned them, to the sound of raucous laughter.

Levity is always welcome in the press room. Duval was addressing the media at the Phoenix Open when the unmistakable sound of flatulence was heard. It happened again and again. Finally, Duval spotted the prankster David Feherty in the back of the room with a whoopie cushion. "I thought it was me for a second," Duval said.

Some memorable exchanges that elicited laughter:

• Nick Faldo was asked what Tiger Woods's presence has meant to the tour. "He hasn't given me any presents," Faldo said.

• Another time, Faldo was asked to assess his swing. "My swing has been like my singing," he said, "a mixture of karaoke and rap. It's called crap."

• After Faldo won the British Open in 1992, he was delivering his victory speech to the Royal and Ancient officers there, when he decided it was an appropriate time to address the tabloid press that had been targeting him. He thanked it "from the heart of my bottom."

• "Do you want a soft drink?" Fuzzy Zoeller was asked as he sat down for an interview. "No, I don't drink," he said. "I'm an athlete." "Something harder?" "Absolut [vodka] and tonic later, please."

• The first time Tiger Woods played in a PGA Tour event was 1992. Sandy Lyle was asked his impression of Tiger Woods. "Tiger Woods?" Sleepy Sandy replied, presumably in jest. "Is that a new golf course?"

Finally, there was Joe Ogilvie, who inadvertently uncovered the truth about the media. He was speaking about the fact that he played twenty-three consecutive weeks, a yeoman's schedule. "It would change a lot," he said, "if I had a family. But I think I'll do it for the foreseeable future. I'm way too immature to get married."

"Aren't we all?" came the reply from a reporter.

10

BEHIND CLOSED DOORS

The locker room is the players' sanctuary, a place to which players can retreat to escape the otherwise ubiquitous autograph hunter. Or so you would think. This was what Tiger Woods assumed when he embarked on his professional career.

Yet when he won the Masters by twelve strokes, his signature became a commodity even among those against whom he was competing. At least autograph requests made by players typically are for the purpose of using them to raise money for a charity, usually in an auction.

Woods's signature is far and away among the most valuable in golf, a burden that he failed to handle with aplomb early on. Billy Andrade and Brad Faxon are hosts of the Charities for Children Tournament, at which they collected $50,000 in 1996 for auctioning a display containing golf balls signed by every living Masters champion. As part of the package, they also promised to provide signed balls from the champions of the subsequent three Masters.

After Woods had won the 1997 Masters, Andrade approached him in the locker room and requested a signed ball. Woods, citing the fact that he does not sign golf balls, summarily rejected Andrade's request. In late 1996 Woods told an International Management Group attorney that he hadn't signed more than a dozen golf balls in the previous three years, yet dozens began turning up in memorabilia stores, an indication that bogus signatures were for sale. Many players, concerned that others are seeking to obtain signed balls for the purpose of turning a profit, do not sign them for fans, but always accommodate other players' requests. Woods, then, had breached unwritten PGA Tour protocol.

Andrade did manage to obtain a signed ball. Two Rhode Island boys, Drew Simmons, eight, and his brother, Dixon, eleven, had attended the U.S. Amateur at Newport Country Club in Newport, Rhode Island, two years earlier, and Woods had signed a ball for each of them. Hearing of Andrade's plight, the boys decided to give up one ball for a worthy cause, donating it to the charity.

Later, Faxon and Davis Love III took Woods aside and explained the rules that maintain a peaceful coexistence in the locker room. It was part of the sharp learning curve to which Woods was subjected, and he has since amended his stance and will sign balls for charitable purposes.

Still, there was a price to pay for his insolence. At the end of the 1998 baseball season, in which Mark McGwire hit a record seventy home runs, the Tiger Woods Foundation attempted to obtain McGwire's autograph for a charity auction. McGwire was said to have declined. Andrade and McGwire have been partners in the AT&T Pebble Beach National Pro-Am, from which a strong friendship evolved.

In defense of Woods, he is inundated by autograph requests. After his Masters victory, he found about one hundred Masters souvenirs in his locker at the Byron Nelson Classic, all of them placed there by fellow PGA Tour players seeking his signature. One player was said to have placed thirty commemorative Masters flags in his locker to sign.

However, the incident with Andrade was not Woods's only locker room oversight. Players are required by the PGA Tour to tip the locker room attendant at least $20 for his services, which include shining shoes. Tips typically are significantly greater than that, depending on a player's benevolence. When Tiger Woods turned pro, among the lessons he was required to learn was that his status among the highest-paid athletes in history required that he tip better than the minimum. He once tipped an attendant $20, to the consternation of one of those in the Woods camp, who from his own money clip augmented the tip with an additional $200.

Of course, Woods was only twenty then, naive and wide-eyed, albeit wealthy with $43 million in endorsement contracts. When he arrived at his locker in the clubhouse at Brown Deer Park Golf Course in Milwaukee to make his professional debut, he marveled at what he found there: three dozen Titleist Tour Balata golf balls and four Titleist golf gloves. "He was like a ten-year-old dropped into the middle of Toys R Us," his teacher Butch Harmon said of a young man who could buy a Toys R Us store.

Each player's locker is stocked with his supply of balls and gloves for the week. Players also tend to find an assortment of notes taped to their lockers, this being the best place for players to communicate with one another.

At the Bay Hill Invitational one year, Davis Love III slammed his wedge against a sprinkler head, breaking it and sending a geyser into the air. When he returned to his locker, he found a repair bill in the sum of $175,003.50, courtesy of the course owner and tournament host, Arnold Palmer.

"The parts were about $3.50," Palmer said later, jokingly. "But I had to have two irrigation engineers, an assistant, and a leading superintendent to get that fixed. That was labor, $175,000."

"That's expensive labor," Love said. "The nice note and bill from Arnold made me feel a lot better. It shows what a classy guy he is."

Actually, the cost to Love was $500, the amount of the fine he was required to pay for conduct unbecoming a professional, and his competitors began calling him "Water Boy." "They keep saying I ought to get a sponsorship deal with Toro [a company that manufactures sprinkler heads]."

The behavior in a golf locker room does not sink to the puerile levels of behavior that exist in baseball locker rooms, which often more closely resemble day-care centers. Still, the practical joke endures there, as it did when Willie Wood took a tube of Super Glue and sealed the pockets on Gary McCord's golf bag.

After Paul Azinger holed a bunker shot at the last hole of the Memorial in 1993 to defeat his friend Payne Stewart by a single stroke, he went to the clubhouse to change his shoes. When he inserted his foot in one, he squashed a peeled banana that had been placed there by Stewart.

A month later, Lee Janzen played so well through the first three rounds of the U.S. Open that a victory seemed imminent, even to him. Azinger and Stewart were close friends, and Janzen was aware of the banana-in-the-shoe prank. On Sunday morning, he posted in his locker a photograph of a banana with a circle drawn around it and a slash through it. The message, intended for Azinger and Stewart, was clear: No banana.

After the final round of the Open, Azinger, who had finished third, and Stewart, the runner-up, sat in the locker room, discussing how well Janzen had played in winning the tournament. Simultaneously, they reached the same conclusion. "Let's put bananas in Janzen's shoes." When they opened his locker, they saw the note that he had put there. They were impressed, though not to a degree that caused them to reconsider their planned high jinks. The banana went into the shoe.

At the GTE Byron Nelson Classic, Nick Price, a native of Zimbabwe, began each day receiving a "Jumbo" tribal dance from Nigerian Martin Oribhabor, the locker-room attendant. Price was seeking good luck, which may or may not have been responsible for his fourth-place finish.

Occasionally, the clubhouse surroundings provide motivation, as they did for Price at Harbor Town Golf Links, site of the MCI Classic, which he won in 1997. The locker room is decorated with posters of past champions. "Arnold Palmer is right in the middle of it," Price said. "Then you look and there's Jack and Hale Irwin. There's a who's who of golf there. I thought it would be really nice to get my face up there as well. Faldo has won here. Langer has won here. Graham Marsh. You don't need to say anything else. Just look at the list."

Rain delays transform the locker room into crowded reading rooms and rest areas, where naps and newspapers are popular. Other diversions included the time Billy Ray Brown bet any and all comers that they couldn't eat four saltine crackers in one minute without an assist from water or any other liquid. None could, and Brown was a big winner.

Paul Goydos was asked how he occupied his time during a particular rain delay. "Well, I played computer golf," he said. "That Latrobe [Country Club] is a tough layout." Asked how he fared, he replied, "Terrible. I can't play that computer golf."

At the Bell Canadian Open, a Sega Bass Fishing game was installed, providing countless mindless hours of entertainment for the tour constituency. "It's a great machine," Phil Blackmar said, "but it always catches a fish. Not that easy in real life."

The clubhouse occasionally is the setting for players' meetings, which frequently are spirited affairs. This is where dirty laundry is aired and issues are debated. At one such meeting prior to the Players Championship in 1999, a committee was formed to study course setups. Originally players said that greens needed to be harder and faster. At this meeting, they said that greens are too firm and fast. "No matter what you do," Davis Love III said, "you can't make everybody happy."

At one meeting, the players were discussing whether the Players Championship ought to be moved from late March to either May or February. Mark Calcavecchia was sitting quietly in the corner, taken aback by what he was hearing. "I almost jumped in and said, 'Look, boys, we're playing for $3.5 million. Who the hell cares when we play?' I'd tee it up in Minneapolis [in the winter] in a snowsuit for $3.5 million."

At another players' meeting, after an unruly fan arrested at the

Phoenix Open was found to have been carrying a gun, security was the issue. It was suggested that fans pass through metal detectors before being permitted on the premises. "It's just not golf," Stewart said of the suggestion. "I just don't see that in golf."

Players at these meetings often complain about media access to the locker room, though the PGA Tour commissioner Tim Finchem and his predecessor Deane Beman have adamantly refused to budge on this issue.

The *Orlando Sentinel* provided fodder for the players' argument when it published something that had been overheard in the locker room rather than something that had been said in an interview. When the NBA suspended the Denver Nuggets' guard Mahmoud Abdul-Rauf for his refusal to stand for the national anthem (he had cited religious reasons), the golfer Mike Sullivan broached the subject in the locker room one day, his words finding their way into the *Orlando Sentinel* the following day.

"I don't think they should suspend him," Sullivan said. "I think they should shoot him."

Later, Sullivan said, "It was an offhand, off-the-cuff comment that was a very poor attempt at humor. It certainly does not reflect my true feelings. I sincerely regret it and apologize for it."

Another time, Brad Faxon was overheard joking about the fact that Jim Gallagher Jr. had skipped the British Open. "I can't believe Jim Gallagher's not here," he said to Davis Love III. "Why would he have a baby the week of the British Open?"

The quote appeared in *USA Today*, as though it had been said in all seriousness. Faxon phone Gallagher and apologized.

These incidents precipitated a players' meeting, in which a growing faction of players called for the banishment of the media from the clubhouse. "Kicking reporters out of the clubhouse won't solve the problem," Faxon wrote in a piece for *Sports Illustrated*. "I like talking to the press and think it's important to be accessible. The problem is, there are getting to be fewer players who agree with me."

Locker rooms remain open to the media, though they are closed to virtually everyone else, club members included. Members typically clean out their lockers and turn them over to the pros for the week the tour is in town. This was the case when the PGA Championship went to Medinah Country Club in Medinah, Illinois, outside Chicago, in 1999.

Mark Brooks discovered that his locker was on loan from one of the club's newest members, who no doubt also would prefer that the media be banned. Brooks was assigned Michael Jordan's locker.

Brooks, incidentally, pledged to leave some balls behind for Jordan. "With this rough," Brooks said, "he'll need them."

11

AFTER HOURS

There was a time when the day ended not at the eighteenth hole, but rather at the nineteenth hole, a favorite gathering place of a vast cross section of touring pros. Here, no one counted the shots.

"Jimmy Demaret and I had the best golf psychologist in the world," the former Masters and PGA Championship winner Jackie Burke said, recalling better days. "His name was Jack Daniels and he was waiting for us after every round."

The old-timers know how to wind down, a trait some apparently carried over onto the Senior PGA Tour. There was the Halloween party into which a couple of the Senior Tour players stumbled at their Universal City hotel during an event in Los Angeles one year. The party was held by the pornographic movie industry, and the costume of choice featured only a few more threads of fabric than are contained in a golf glove.

"I never missed a tee time in my life," one of the players in attendance said while observing the surroundings, "but I might miss one tomorrow."

Neon was the guiding light of generations past.

"The young guys today go to their hotel, have an iced tea," the occasional tippler Fuzzy Zoeller said. "It's a horrible way to live, but my hat's off to them. The fact that I've seen guys stone-cold drunk beat guys stone-cold sober tells you what kind of game golf is."

It's a funny game, as the golfer said to the caddy.
Yeah, but it wasn't meant to be, the caddy replied.

This, of course, was why nineteenth-hole therapy once was so popular. That does not remain the case, which points to the changing nature of a game that no longer is simply a game. Golf now is a business as well, big business, with enormous stakes that preclude most players from keeping late hours that occasionally collide with early tee times. The depth of talent is such that the player who routinely arrives at the first tee with a headache is not likely to have the opportunity to do so on the PGA Tour for long.

So what do players do with the vast blocks of down time that a life on the road provides them?

John Daly eats. Asked what he would do in the aftermath of his shooting a surprising 68 in the first round of the U.S. Open at Pinehurst, Daly replied, "I'm going to go eat about six cheeseburgers at McDonald's, probably have a bag of Oreos, and a big thing of milk, watch *SportsCenter*, and hopefully see myself on TV."

He also gambles, to extremes that have proved costly, though he once left a blackjack table with $187,500 in winnings. "Usually he wants to sit there until they name the place after him," one of his managers, Bud Martin, said. "He's shown a lot of discipline to walk away this time."

The modern players' nineteenth hole has stationary bicycles and stair climbers. Even Daly at one time went on a fitness kick, however reluctantly. In the fall of 1998, he lost thirty-eight pounds, reducing his weight to two-twenty, though he was never likely to write a diet-and-fitness book. "I hate every minute of it," he said. "I'm not sure I can stick with it. I hate it. I can't stand working out. I'm hoping my addictive nature will help me. Maybe I'll get addicted to working out."

The most popular place to work out on the PGA Tour is the fitness van that follows the tour and parks at the tournament site. The van measures forty-eight feet long and is a state-of-the-art fitness facility driven from town to town by one of the physical therapists employed by the tour to assist players.

Fitness has become an obsession on the tour, in no small measure as a result of Tiger Woods's dominance. Woods is a frequent visitor to the fitness trailer or a local health club, ensuring that the cheeseburgers so prevalent in his daily diet don't cause the scales to tip against him. Others already have to spot Woods an advantage in talent and distance; they don't want him to have an additional advantage because he is more physically fit. So they exercise. Even Craig Stadler, the Walrus, decided that extra-large was a size that the PGA Tour no longer could accommodate successfully; he arrived for the 2000 season having shed thirty-five pounds.

Not everyone has embraced this lifestyle, of course. An off-season when his caloric intake was not offset by enough exercise caused Steve Pate to travel to the Mercedes Championship with some excess baggage that he was eager to discard. He showed up in the fitness trailer one afternoon and asked, "Do you have liposuction in here?"

They had everything else, including a multistation gym, treatment tables, therapists, and a television set, perhaps only the latter holding much appeal to Pate. *Golf Digest's* writer Bob Verdi remarked to Pate that many golfers have become physical fitness fanatics, that their bodies are their temples. "I understand," Pate replied. "I just don't worship mine as much."

Tim Herron is known as Lumpy for apparent reasons, and he is not an aficionado of the fitness arts. His routine is five minutes on the stationary bike to loosen up. "If I really got tired of it," he said of the nickname, "I'd stop eating and start exercising."

Perhaps shedding weight would disturb his ballast and ruin his swing. As for nutrition, he facetiously notes the advantages of a big breakfast.

"I've got a different idea about tempo," he said. "The key is a big, big breakfast, lots of pancakes, sausages, and eggs. I get all that breakfast in me, and I get real slowed down and that helps me have a slower and smoother tempo."

Herron walked into the fitness trailer one day. "Do you want to stretch?" he was asked.

"Nope," Herron replied. "No need to stretch fat."

Some players prefer moving at a clip substantially faster than what a treadmill can do. These are the thrill seekers on the PGA Tour. At the Las Vegas Invitational, Phil Mickelson and Fred Couples ventured north to Mesquite, Nevada, to ride the renowned roller coaster there.

Woods is among a handful of PGA Tour players who have hitched a thrill ride of another sort, aboard a fighter jet. When he was playing in the Las Vegas Invitational one year, Woods went up in an Air Force Thunderbird jet, which reached speeds in excess of five hundred seventy miles during the thirty-five-minute flight. "I'd love to do it again," he said.

Of course he would. There are no crowds in the wild blue yonder. Woods's movements away from the course are restricted by his celebrity. At the AT&T Pebble Beach National Pro-Am, he was getting a haircut at the Pebble Beach Salon after the second round and people peered through the window at him, as though he were standing over a crucial putt on the eighteenth green. One woman even entered the shop later, seeking to obtain a handful of discarded locks. At the Western Open, he and Mark O'Meara had to enter via the back door of the Oak Brook Cinema, when they went to see *Men in Black*, starring Woods's friend Will Smith. "I wouldn't want to be Tiger Woods," O'Meara said. "I can still go to the Olive Garden and have dinner and nobody bothers me."

One night, O'Meara, his wife Alicia, and Woods went to a McDonald's, a five-star restaurant by Woods's definition. The girl behind the counter recognized Woods and shrieked. "Scared the living daylights out of me," O'Meara said. O'Meara, naturally, went unrecognized.

Obscurity has its downside as well. O'Meara occasionally is mistaken for Mark McCumber, another PGA Tour player with a receding hairline. At least he is recognized as a golfer at such times, unlike the first time he arrived at the gate of the Sahalee Country Club in Redmond, Washington, for the PGA Championship in 1998. O'Meara was the reigning Masters and British Open champion at the time, and he was with Woods. "Welcome to Sahalee, Mr. Woods," the police officer stationed there said. "We're sure happy to have you here. Hope you play well and enjoy your stay." The officer then turned to O'Meara. "Can I help you, sir?" he asked.

The commotion Woods causes is an inducement for him to remain in at night. The popular video game *Mortal Kombat* and table tennis occupied Woods's nights during the Masters in 1997, pastimes that illustrated the generation gap between him and the golf world he was on the brink of conquering.

The ballpark or arena is a popular night spot for PGA Tour types. Charlie Rymer enjoyed a Texas Rangers game from a luxury box at The Ballpark at Arlington following the second round of the GTE Byron Nelson Classic, and he reinforced his two-hundred-forty-pound frame by feasting on the smorgasbord laid out for him and his friends. The following morning he had a $23 breakfast at the Four Seasons in Irving, Texas, then went out and flirted with a 59, before settling for a 61 in a round in which his putts "looked like rats running into holes out there. I was thinking 59," he said, though he recognized that he would need a modified nickname, since Al Geiberger already is known as Mr. 59. "I was going to be 'Fat Mr. 59.'"

Game tickets often are provided free by tournament hosts. Sam Torrance, born in Scotland and a resident of England, was in the

United States for the Masters and was playing at New Orleans in a tune-up. He received a ticket to the New York Yankees–Boston Red Sox exhibition game at New Orleans's Superdome and came away with a less than favorable impression of America's national pastime.

"It was long," he said of a game won by the Red Sox, 16–11.

Craig Stadler, an inveterate hockey fan, often went to Los Angeles Kings games at the Great Western Forum during the Nissan Open and is a friend and occasional golfing partner of Wayne Gretzky. David Duval threw out the ceremonial first pitch three times one season, even taking batting practice before a Mets-Marlins game one year. Billy Andrade and his wife, Jody, were guests of Blue Jays pitcher Roger Clemens during a game at the Sky Dome in Toronto during the Bell Canadian Open in 1998. Andrade later won the tournament.

Other players prefer the participatory sports. The B.C. Open in Endicott, New York, is home to an annual pickup hockey game. The B.C. Open is a throwback tournament, though not necessarily as a result of the Johnny Hart caveman cartoon after which the tournament was named. The B.C. Open has no corporate sponsor and no leader boards; this gives it a cozy feel. For many players, it is a welcome respite from the cookie-cutter type of tournament. Players also come for the annual Saturday night hockey game at a local rink.

Patrick Burke has been a regular, and the team for which he plays is generally favored. Burke's passion is hockey, a game he played reasonably well through high school. He even played in the pickup game at the B.C. Open in 1996, when he was entering the final round in third place with a chance to win.

"The way I am," said Burke, whose golf career has been marred by injuries, "I can get hurt eating. Hockey is still my first love. I came here to skate."

Burke's team won that year, 30–10, which points to the players' inexperience in stopping another's shot. Golfers don't play defense. Burke was the star, but Brad Faxon contributed, once he located a protective cup. He had forgotten to pack his and was able to locate only junior cups, "and that certainly wouldn't do," Faxon said. Eventually, he found an XL, and the game was on.

When the Mercedes Championship moved from Carlsbad, California, to Maui in 1999, Davis Love III had an opportunity to take up surfing. He was coached by two surfing legends: Buzzy Kerbox and Hans Hedeman.

Fuzzy Zoeller's chronic back problems preclude him from participating in bone-rattling endeavors. He often spends downtime attempting to relieve pain of one sort or another. At the Players Championship in 1996, he was attempting to relieve pain in the knuckle of the ring finger on his right hand and concluded, perhaps, that laughter was the best medicine. "Had a calcium deposit that had grown on the knuckle," he explained. "It's gotten very, very sore. That's a step right before old age, I think. You heard about the two guys that went and bought flowers? The one guy bought flowers for his wife. You didn't hear that one? Other guy said, 'God, those are beautiful chrysanthemums.' Guy said, 'Hey, those aren't chrysanthemums; those are roses.' He said, 'No, those are chrysanthemums.' He said, 'Well, then, how do you spell chrysanthemums?' He said, 'By God, they are roses.'"

Laughter, however, failed to relieve the pain as effectively as acupuncture, a treatment he received during the tournament. "I've had a lot done to that finger," he said. "Let's see, I had cortisone. I've had a voodoo guy come over and do a dance on it, had acupuncture done to it. Right down there on James Butler and I–95. I'll try anything once. Five [needles] on the knuckle and two on the ends. It's not that bad. A cup of coffee and a good newspaper, it's all over with in twenty minutes.

"I'll probably have another shot of acupuncture [later in the week]. It's the neatest little thing. He brings in this little bag all full of needles and he just goes, 'Psst, psst, psst.' It is the cat's meow."

The one post-golf activity in which Zoeller will zealously participate is possibly the most popular diversion for the PGA Tour
player, fishing. Some players are so passionate about fishing that
they seemingly would rather land the trophy fish than the trophy.
In the PGA Tour Media Guide, each player's special interests are
listed, and fishing is nearly universal. Bruce Lietzke's variation on
this theme is that his special interest is "serious fishing." Greg
Norman returned from a layoff once and was asked what it was
that he was working on. "I'm just working on trying to get the reel
action out of my swing," he said, demonstrating a cast.

So it is not surprising that once golf has concluded for the day
during tournament week, many players repair to the ponds, which
pull double duty for them, serving as water hazards in the morning, fishing holes in the afternoon.

The lakes on the Stadium Course at the TPC at Sawgrass in
Ponte Vedra, Florida, are a popular post-round destination during
the Players Championship each March. The tournament keeps a
supply of rods and reels in the clubhouse for the players' use,
though many players travel with their own equipment.

Phil Blackmar and Mike Hulbert are among the incurable of
the tour's outdoor set who frequent the ponds. Hulbert is considered the best fisherman on tour, one that bass fishing guide Pete
Matson said was the only PGA Tour player good enough to com-
pete as a professional bass fisherman. Johnny Miller, there as an
NBC broadcaster, also frequents the ponds on the property.
Zoeller, Tom Watson, and Justin Leonard occasionally wet a line
as well.

The lakes are stocked and during tournament week are reserved
for the exclusive use of the PGA Tour players, who cast for large-
mouth bass that range up to ten pounds. It is strictly catch and
release. "We haven't had anyone bring one up to the chef yet,"

said Billy Reid, director of golf there and the brother of PGA Tour player Mike Reid. "Notice I said 'yet.'"

The pond adjacent to the putting green at Sawgrass is one of the more popular fishing holes. Payne Stewart was an avid fishermen, who would commandeer a cart and head toward the end of a large lake adjacent to the path leading from the ninth green to the back of eighteen.

The alligators that lurk in the ponds have not represented a problem, though a caddy once dipped his white towel to wet it down and had it snatched away by a gator. Nor has anyone suffered a fate similar to that of one of the goats originally kept at the course to keep the rough and the fescue grasses down. "The goat was walking near the putting green," Billy Reid said, "and became half a goat. That was not a good deal."

Fishing is so popular among PGA Tour players that when officials of the Doral-Ryder Open decided to discontinue the annual fishing derby it held for them, they protested, and the contest was reinstated. The event did not proceed without a dose of controversy, however good-natured. Andy Bean landed a bass that was thought to have been a winner, only for officials to realize it had been weighed on an improper scale. In fact, Blaine McCallister had hooked a larger bass, four pounds ten ounces. The solution was to declare them cowinners, each of them receiving the first prize of having their hotel room at Doral comped.

"That's an eight-hundred-dollar fish I caught," McCallister said, regarding his room savings. "This is an official win, but it's not a major. Disney is the big one. But I think this win gets me in the Masters, doesn't it?"

Bob Verdi wrote in *Golf World* magazine: "Understand that if there's an official food of the PGA Tour, it has to be fish. Wherever this road show travels now, the 19th hole isn't about martinis anymore. If I were a fish, I'd swim upstream as soon as the golfers hit town. In fact, if it weren't for fish, there might not even be a PGA Tour."

Tom Lehman is a deeply religious man who on occasion has been the guest speaker at a local house of worship. One such occasion came during the Masters in 1994, when he led after the third round and on the morning of the final round spoke at the United Methodist Church about a mile from Augusta National. There was no divine intervention this time. He finished second to Jose Maria Olazabal.

Early in the week of the Tour Championship in Tulsa, Oklahoma, in 1996, Lehman fared better. He spoke at the Woodland Acres Baptist Church, a few miles from Southern Hills, and attracted a crowd of about one thousand. A week later, he won the tournament.

Steve Elkington practiced putting for three hours in his hotel room on the morning of the final round of the Players Championship. He watched *Daylight*, a Sylvester Stallone movie, that morning before leaving for the golf course. Several hours later, he won handily.

Often only a quiet dinner is on a player's post-golf agenda, as it was for Justin Leonard one year at the Phoenix Open. Virtually nothing went right for him one day. "I didn't drive back to the hotel," he said. "I let somebody drive me, because I didn't want anything else to happen. I didn't leave the room, actually. I didn't want to trip and fall downstairs or get in a car accident."

The pizza he had delivered to his room?

"Slide it under the door," he told the pizza man.

12

SHOW UP, KEEP UP, AND SHUT UP

The tenuous hold a caddy has on a bag is not the result of forty or fifty pounds of deadweight slung over his shoulder. His is a job without a quantifiable contribution, or even an identifiable contribution in some cases. Cut to the quick, he totes luggage for a living.

Only a Los Angeles jury could conclude that Tiger Woods's success was due in any part to the man toting his bag. Woods, in fact, could pack his own bag and win a tournament, as he did in college not that long ago. As a professional, Woods has won with three different caddies, including a student at the University of California medical school, Bryon Bell, who in his professional debut won with Woods, at the Buick Invitational in 1999. It isn't brain surgery, as Dr. Bell himself is qualified to note.

Woods employed Bell, a boyhood friend, again two weeks later at the WGC Anderson Consulting Match Play Championship, fueling speculation that Mike Cowan's tenure as Woods's caddy was nearing an end after a thirty-month run. Woods attempted to explain that he was simply taking an opportunity to help a friend with his considerable medical school tuition, a noble undertaking if it was true. Woods earned upwards of $30 million in prize and endorsement money in 1999 and could have paid Bell's entire tuition, room, and board with a single flourish of his pen.

It was, in fact, the end of the Woods-Cowan pairing, for reasons that were never fully explained. One suspicion was that Cowan's own growing celebrity was unwelcome to Woods. Or, put more bluntly, Cowan had become too big for his britches.

This would not have been the first time a caddy attempted to step out from an imposing shadow to take bows of his own only to be told he was not welcome back. Arnold Palmer was said to have fired his Masters caddy, Nathanial Avery, when Avery began describing his relationship with Palmer as a corporation, "Arnie and me." "There's room for only one prima donna," Palmer often said. He might have been speaking on behalf of his future brethren in the fraternity of stardom.

Cowan had become golf's most recognizable caddy, in part because of his bushy mustache and fitting nickname; he is known universally in golf circles as Fluff. Yet his renown grew because he was Woods's bag man. Remember, he had the same nickname and bushy mustache when he caddied for another popular player, Peter Jacobsen, for several years without garnering the attention he did in Woods's employ.

Somehow, Fluff's autograph became a commodity, and he routinely obliged those thrusting pen and paper at him. He also filmed commercials for ESPN and for a motel chain, and he agreed to do an instructional video.

Even Curtis Strange wondered whether Cowan had overstepped his bounds. "I don't know if he was doing his job to the best of his ability," Strange wrote in his *Golf* magazine column. "I do know that a caddy signing autographs and doing commercials can be distracting to a player. If those activities weigh on a player—even a little—the relationship can be severely hurt."

One is left to wonder why it would be a distraction, particularly for a player who publicly professes a desire to have the attention paid to him diverted elsewhere. Then again, when that attention is diverted elsewhere to someone basking in Woods's reflected glory, that might be another matter.

Ego is a peculiar commodity.

Cowan quickly found another employer, Jim Furyk, who is among the more consistent players on the PGA Tour, and one on whom a caddy can depend to earn a respectable living, even a lucrative one, without having to endure the hysteria that surrounds Tiger Woods. All it essentially requires is punctuality. Furyk had fired his caddy of nearly five years, Steve Duplantis, who apparently was tardy too often, though he was given several chances to reform. Indeed, other caddies reckoned he was fireproof and accordingly dubbed him Asbestos.

Asbestos, meanwhile, went to work for Rich Beem and immediately demonstrated his historical shortcoming as a caddy. Prior to the final round of the Kemper Open, Duplantis phoned Beem to inform him that he had locked his car keys and his room key in his hotel and that he was running late. "He showed up two minutes after I got on the driving range," Beem said. "I was never worried. I knew he was going to be here no matter what." Later that day, Beem was celebrating his first PGA Tour victory and crediting Duplantis with an assist.

So it goes. So it went for Cowan, who discovered yet again that the workload is the same, whoever is writing the check. "Hey, man, there are tees, there are greens, and there are holes," Cowan said, when at the Masters he was asked to comment on the change. "It's still golf."

And caddies are still caddies, part of a nomadic tribe of blue-collar workers whose value to their employer is the subject of an endless debate.

Ernie Els was asked what he wants from a caddy. "Someone who turns up at the first tee on time and sober," he said. This is a variation of the old Jack Nicklaus theme regarding what he expects from caddies: He wants them to "show up, keep up, and shut up."

Nicklaus might have been the best in history at managing his way around a golf course, and he required no advice from one who knew considerably less than he did. Just as Lee Trevino said he would not hire an instructor until he found one who could beat him, Nicklaus eschewed seeking advice from a man who carried a golf bag for a living.

Yet who could argue that Jean Van de Velde would not have benefited from an experienced caddy imploring him, coercing him, even *ordering* him, to lay up at the seventy-second hole of the British Open, even refusing to relinquish the 2-iron and offering him only a 9-iron, take it or leave it?

At that point in time, Van de Velde required an experienced caddy, and instead he had an inexperienced yes-man, who stood by and watched his meal ticket self-destruct. Eventually, Van de Velde fired the man, too late to secure the Claret Jug that by rights should have been his. Van de Velde's consolation prize? He was dubbed the Claret Jughead by the *Atlanta Journal-Constitution*'s golf writer Glenn Sheeley.

Jerry Pate, meanwhile, won the U.S. Open at the Atlanta Athletic Club in 1976 when his caddy, John Considine, talked him out of hitting a 4-iron second shot to the eighteenth green in the final round, instead recommending the 5-iron. Pate was concerned that a 5-iron would not be enough club for him to clear the pond fronting the green. Considine eventually prevailed, and Pate hit a 5-iron second shot to within three feet of the hole, leading to a birdie that enabled him to win by two strokes.

This was one example of an experienced caddy's paying dividends. Rocco Mediate offered another. In July of 1998, he hired Pete Bender, whose résumé included stints with Greg Norman, Raymond Floyd, Ian Baker-Finch, and John Cook, each of whom won with Bender on his bag.

Early on, when Mediate was missing a plethora of putts, Bender analyzed his charge's game and reached an unflattering conclusion.

"You're not ready to win yet," Bender told him.

"Really," Mediate replied. "Tell me something I don't know."

"I'll tell you when you're ready to win," Bender said.

At the Bob Hope Chrysler Classic early in 1999, Mediate finished twenty-fifth, and Bender interpreted this as a powerful portent. Mediate had begun to hole putts that he previously had been missing.

"Now you're ready," Bender told Mediate.

The next time out, the Phoenix Open, Mediate outplayed Tiger Woods down the stretch and won for the first time in six years.

"When you're on the bag with guys who have won twenty-some-odd events, they know what they're doing," Mediate said. "There's umpteen shots he saved me. He had said, 'Phoenix and Pebble Beach and L.A., that's you. That's where we're going to do something.' I don't know that. But he's been around. I told him walking up eighteen, 'Without you this isn't happening.' He denies that, of course. But he's been around thirty years. He knows what the hell is going on. He acted like today was a practice round. He's helped me tremendously. Some guys don't need that. I love it, though. I like to be out there with someone as a team."

These are the kinds of relationships from which the caddy clearly earns his substantial keep, which, if past percentages hold, meant that Bender had earned ten percent of Mediate's $540,000 take, or $54,000. For carrying a golf bag.

Larry Mize is among those who won't fault their caddies for their own mistakes. Mize bogeyed the eighteenth hole in the final round of the Canon Greater Hartford Open in 1998, costing himself a victory. Standing in the fairway, he was between clubs, 5-iron or 4-iron; opted for the latter; and hit his approach shot over the green.

"He [the caddy] thought four, too, so we're both in the dog-house," Mize said. "No, I never blame my caddy. I pull the club. I'm the boss. I pulled the wrong club."

A good caddy helps earn his keep by knowing where the television cameras are located and when they are likely to be pointed at his man and when the red light is on. When Fred Couples represented Lynx during the most productive years of his career, Lynx executives loved the job Couples's caddy, Joe LaCava, did on the company's behalf. LaCava, they said, was an expert at ensuring that the large Lynx logo on Couples's bag was facing the television camera that was pointed at the player.

The beer money for which caddies used to work has in some instances become champagne money. The typical arrangement is for the caddy to receive a weekly stipend, around $700, as well as five percent of the player's earnings, seven percent of his earnings should he finish in the top ten, and ten percent of his earnings for a victory. Given that most tournaments now offer in excess of $500,000 to the winner, the stakes have risen dramatically.

The arrangement Woods has with his new caddy, Steve Williams, has not been revealed, but in all likelihood calls for Williams to receive a flat salary, with bonuses, perhaps. If Williams was operating on the percentage system, he'd have earned $100,000 for Woods's victory at the WGC-NEC Invitational and another $100,000 for his victory at the WGC–American Express Championship. Given that Woods won six other PGA Tour events, Williams would have made more money than many of those golfers finishing in the top one-twenty-five on the PGA Tour money list.

The changing economics have strained some relationships. Players began questioning whether a caddy was worth the kind of money one would make toting the bag for a star-caliber player. Some players have opted to pay their caddies an annual salary in lieu of a percentage that might have made some of them wealthy men in a matter of a few years.

Speculation was that Mark O'Meara fired Jerry Higginbotham in part because the boss had concluded he did not need a caddy who was costing him $200,000 or more a year. O'Meara stated flatly that he had no intention of ever again paying a caddy ten percent of a winning purse.

Higginbotham, incidentally, had the dubious distinction of getting fired twice in one year. When O'Meara fired him, it appeared as though O'Meara had unwittingly done him a favor, relieving him of any commitment he might have had to an old warhorse, freeing him to hook up with a young thoroughbred. O'Meara is forty-three and in the waning years of a productive career. Higginbotham was hired by the Spanish prodigy Sergio Garcia, nineteen at the time and destined to win frequently over the next twenty-five years, enabling his caddy to live a life of luxury as well.

Higginbotham joined Garcia at the Byron Nelson Classic, where Garcia finished third, hinting at the potential the Spaniard possessed. The union lasted less than a year. The first public sign of trouble came at the WGC–American Express Championship in Valderrama later in the year. Garcia struggled with his club selection at the par-3 sixth hole, eventually choosing an 8-iron that did not elicit a confident reaction from Higginbotham. Garcia's shot landed fifteen yards short of the green.

"I think that was the wrong club," Garcia said, his sarcasm directed toward Higginbotham. "I don't know, but I'm pretty sure that's short."

The following week, Higginbotham failed to recognize that Garcia was about to take an illegal drop in the final round of the Taiheiyo Masters in Japan. Garcia took the drop and later was assessed a two-stroke penalty. A week later, Garcia informed Higginbotham that he was fired.

A caddy's value to a player obviously varies, but the fact is that he (or she) carries a bag for a living. Caddies then are tantamount to porters, though this is not meant to disparage the hard work they do. The point is that none of them is indispensable. "I don't know a single caddy who will win or lose a tournament this year,"

Strange wrote. "But we're acting as if players can't possibly hit a shot without a high-profile, highly paid caddy."

Ouch.

The truth sometimes hurts, of course. The men who finished first, second, and third at the Greater Greensboro Open in 1999 each had a new caddy that week.

"The tour caddies took a hit," Scott Hoch said jokingly.

Jeff Maggert, who finished third, was using his girlfriend, Michelle Austin, a resident of Greensboro, a rank amateur. "The first time she ever caddied was on Tuesday," Maggert said. "I was kind of showing her the caddy etiquette, so to speak. She's been great. I always say a good caddy is a caddy that you never see, and that means that they're staying out of everyone's way."

Jeff Manson caddied that week for his college teammate, Jim Furyk, who finished second. The winner, meanwhile, was Jesper Parnevik, whose caddy was Lance Ten Broeck, a veteran PGA Tour pro, who earned $46,800, the second largest check of his career. He questioned the sum he was paid, even as he acknowledged that he needed the money. "I think it's way too much money," he said. "I can't see paying a caddy ten percent. He's not that important."

Parnevik was not inclined to argue. When he was informed that the top three all had new caddies, he replied, "Maybe that's the key."

Ernie Els dismissed Ric Roberts, the man who was on his bag for his two U.S. Open victories, when it was evident they had grown weary of one another's company. "We've had some great times together, won a lot of big tournaments, including two U.S. Opens," Els said. "But last year we started to irritate each other. I just think I need a change of caddy, a fresh person on the bag."

John Burke, affectionately known as Cubby, caddied for a long time for Brad Faxon, one of the more affable players on tour, which might explain how Burke stuck around as long as he did.

Faxon was penalized for playing the wrong ball twice in one year. Part of the caddy's job is to ensure that that does not happen. Once, Faxon and Phil Mickelson were using identical Titleist balls and mixed them up. The other time, Burke handed a different model of Titleist ball to Faxon, who failed to notice the difference and played it, in violation of the rules.

On rare occasions, the caddy has been responsible for severing ties, in effect firing the boss. Dave Renwick was on Jose Maria Olazabal's bag when the Spaniard won the Masters in 1994, but a few weeks later informed him that he was going to work elsewhere. His decision was said to have been based on inadequate pay as well as the verbal abuse to which he was subjected. He found another loop with Vijay Singh, who won the PGA Championship in 1998 with Renwick at his side.

Cowan, in fact, left his boss to join Woods. When Woods turned pro in 1996, Cowan's player of nineteen years, Peter Jacobsen, was nursing a sore back and did not intend to play much the remainder of the year. At Jacobsen's suggestion, Cowan went to work on a temporary basis for Woods, who required a veteran tour caddy in his bid to earn PGA Tour playing privileges in a limited amount of time.

When it became evident that Woods possessed the ability and the desire to deliver on his potential, Cowan informed Jacobsen that he was leaving him to work full-time for Woods.

The latest caddy to dump a player was Fanny Sunesson, who late in 1999 informed Nick Faldo that their ten-year relationship was over. Sunesson was on Faldo's bag for four of his six major championships, but a prolonged slump by an aging Faldo had dramatically diminished her earning power. At the same time, Sergio Garcia, the nineteen-year-old phenom from Spain, had fired his new caddy, Higginbotham, leading to speculation that Sunesson saw an opportunity to discard a well that had run dry in favor of one expected to gush. Sunesson later went to work for Garcia.

"Our success is well documented," Sunesson told Golf.com,

regarding her years with Faldo, "and I know it will be difficult to attain anything like it elsewhere. Nick has been very understanding of my decision, which has been extremely tough to make. However, I feel the time is now right for me to move on."

Sunesson, it should be noted, used the modifier *our* in discussing Faldo's success, the caddy's term for attaching importance to the job. Nowhere did she talk about Faldo's slump by saying "our failure."

In defense of tour caddies, they have what generally is a thankless job. When a player has to vent, the caddy is his most visible target and often bears the brunt of the anger. Caddies have to carry a bag that weighs in excess of forty pounds, up and down hills, more than four hours a day in a variety of uncomfortable weather conditions, and their take-home pay depends entirely on the fickle nature of a game that, even played at the highest level, is frustrating at best. They are required to pay their own travel expenses and buy their own health insurance.

They are second-class citizens in the golf world, recognized as such even by the PGA Tour, which notes in its *Player Handbook and Tournament Regulations* that "Caddies may NOT use player locker rooms. Players whose caddies enter the locker rooms initially will be fined $100. Subsequent fines during a year will be $250 and $500 respectively."

For years the caddies have asked that they be permitted to wear shorts on hot days, yet the PGA Tour declined, until a caddy collapsed in the heat at the Western Open in 1999.

Jeff Maggert recognizes the plight of the caddy and gladly paid his man, Brian Sullivan, the standard ten percent when he won $1 million at the WGC–Andersen Consulting Match Play championship. "It's good to see caddies reap some benefits," Maggert said. "They've been treated poorly, like second-class citizens, for too long."

Those on the fringe, without a star benefactor, understand this better than most. They have been known to save money by bunking in the van in which they travel, then joining a local health club for a week, providing themselves a place to work out and shower. Often a pair of guest badges to the tournament could be bartered for the weekly gym dues.

Caddy Steve Hulka once wrote in *The Official Caddy Guide*, a weekly newsletter for the benefit of tour caddies, that he developed a side business, detailing amateur participants' cars during pro-am day. "It only takes an hour per car and no water," he wrote. "Two towels and Dri Wash 'n' Guard is all you need. I did seven cars in Phoenix at $20 per car in the time it takes to loop on Wednesday."

The key, then, is finding a consistent moneymaker and toeing the line, however that is defined. A violation of the "shut up" part of Nicklaus's equation has cost many a caddy a job. On the second hole of the final round of the Shell Houston Open, the caddy Paul Jungman implored his man, Fred Funk, to bear down, admonishing him for failing to demonstrate the requisite intensity.

"When he said that," Funk said, "that was it."

The basis for their disagreement occurred moments before the fateful round began. Funk was joking with a life-size cutout of David Duval, a gesture that apparently was interpreted by Jungman as a lack of focus. After Jungman voiced his opinion, "I spent the next three holes cussing him and played those holes four over," Funk said. "After a while, I told him not to talk to me anymore, and I told him after the round that we were done."

Three weeks later, at the Colonial, Funk's caddy was his wife, Sharon, who was two and a half months pregnant at the time.

Fuzzy Zoeller had employed Mike Mazzeo for eighteen years, when the latter showed up late for work one day. Zoeller asked for an explanation. "He said, 'I'm on a work slowdown. I haven't been making much money lately,'" Zoeller said.

Zoeller's response: "Well, you're making even less now." He fired him on the spot.

Fulton Allem was three over par through fourteen holes at the MCI Classic once, a dispiriting round that piqued his anger.

"What should I break?" he asked his caddy, a man who answers to Bullet.

"How about par?" Bullet replied, presumably as part of his resignation speech.

The fate of Jose Manual Carriles's caddy, who left his charge's 7-iron behind at the twelfth hole one day, is uncertain. Two holes later, Carriles had a 7-iron shot, but no 7-iron. His caddy retraced his steps, finally finding the club. By the time he handed it to Carriles, Carriles had been slapped with a two-stroke penalty for delaying play. He missed the cut by a single shot.

Andrew Magee was on the threshold of winning for the first time as a professional at the Pensacola Open in 1988, and he faced a crucial putt on the seventeenth hole. His caddy that week was a stand-in, one he never used before or after, and one who could smell a lucrative payday. "I had a ten-foot par putt on seventeen," Magee recalled. "He hadn't said a word to me all week. He goes, 'You better make this one, pro.' That's all he said." Magee made it and went on to win the tournament.

Siblings or spouses employed as caddies tend to have greater job security, though they are not infallible. Mike Springer has the dubious distinction of having fired his twin brother, Marty, who caddied for Springer the first three months of his professional career. "His mind really wasn't there," Springer said, "and I had to fire him. I just told him it wasn't working out and I needed to make some changes. He understood. He went home and went back to work."

Marty Springer asked that he be given another chance some day. Eight years later, Springer severed ties with his caddy, Dave Begley, and rehired Marty.

The sibling or spouse as caddy creates curious, though not unusual, dynamics. In any given tournament, at least one player probably has his wife carrying his bag, its cumbersome weight notwithstanding. Steve Stricker's wife, Nicki, served as his full-time caddy until her pregnancy reached a point where continuing to do so represented an unnecessary health risk.

Skip Kendall's wife, Beth, used to caddy for him. "Out there I call the shots," he said, "but I'm pretty sure it's the other way around most places."

The temperamental Ken Green employed his sister Shelley to caddy for him at the Masters once, and he opened the tournament with a 68 that left everyone in a good mood. A second-round 78 restored irritability. The joke making the rounds in the press room was that the only green Ken hit all day was his sister. Green, incidentally, later fired his sister and hired their cousin, Joe LaCava, who eventually went to work full-time for Fred Couples.

John Huston pressed his sister, Julie Jones, into service for a single week at the United Airlines Hawaiian Open in 1998 and set a tour record for strokes under par—twenty-eight—in a seventy-two-hole event. "She never said one word to me all week," Huston said. "She was scared stiff." She nearly fainted in the midst of Tuesday's practice round, the burden of the bag and the hot, humid weather nearly proving too much.

Mark Calcavecchia frequently has used his wife, Sheryl, as his caddy. An aerobics instructor and fitness fanatic, Sheryl easily wielded the weighty bag around a golf course. Tom Lehman, meanwhile, pressed his wife, Melissa, into service at the Nissan Open in 1998, when his regular caddy, Andy Martinez, broke two ribs in a pickup basketball game on the eve of the tournament. Melissa demanded that Tom lose the heavy tour bag and replace it with a considerably lighter carry bag, or Sunday bag.

A loud vote against the wife or girlfriend doubling as a caddy was registered by Australia's Wayne Riley, who caught a bad lie in a bunker that a caddy apparently had neglected to rake at the Scottish Open on the European PGA Tour. Riley then voiced a complaint against players who use wives or girlfriends to caddy for them, implying that they are unaware of their obligations as caddies, of which raking bunkers is one. He angrily took a swing at the face of the bunker, for which he was fined two hundred fifty pounds. "Why," an indignant Riley said, "don't you double it?" The tour agreed and increased the amount to five hundred pounds.

Davis Love III, Bob Tway, Steve Jones, and Chip Beck are among players who have used their brothers as full-time caddies.

Golf Digest's writer Tom Callahan suggested that small light-weight carry bags be banned from major championships, that all players be required to use the hefty tour bag as a hedge against overzealous relatives making a spectacle of themselves, as Peter Kuchar did caddying for his amateur son Matt at the U.S. Open. "Under the strain," Callahan wrote, "they're bound to be a little less animated down the stretch." Peter Kuchar resembled a cheerleader, and Matt's playing partners found this to be a distraction.

Scott Simpson once used a friend, actor-comedian Bill Murray, to caddy for him at the Western Open. Murray abandoned Simpson at the seventy-second and final hole, leaving his charge to tote his own bag down the eighteenth fairway. "My only concern," Simpson said, "is that he gets too good at this and Fluff is out of a job."

The following year, Murray left a message for Simpson. "He told me he couldn't make it this year because his mother wanted him to clean out the garage," Simpson said.

It is apparent that Simpson is among those players capable of fending for themselves rather than relying on a caddy's experience or expertise, or his ability to say the right words at the right time. Indeed, a year after employing a comedian, Simpson hired a quarterback to carry his bag, Stan Humphries of the San Diego Chargers. Humphries, a veteran quarterback adept at withstanding a heavy rush and throwing a touchdown pass, confessed that he was more nervous than Simpson and decided he might best help him by staying out of his way. Simpson won the Buick Invitational with Humphries on his bag.

It also would behoove a caddy not to threaten to kill his boss. "It was Mother's Day of '96," R. W. Eaks said. "I was getting a lift to the airport from a caddy, who was going to go to work for me, and we were in the wrong lane, and he decided to cross six lanes, and we didn't quite make it. A lady hit us from the back, and the truck went airborne and flipped over, and we skidded about four hundred fifty feet, because we were going about sixty-five, and she was going about ninety."

Did the caddy get the job?

"No," Eaks replied. "Actually I haven't talked to him since then. I was kind of instructed not to talk to him for a while, and he's doing something else now."

The caddy's metaphor may have been delivered by a large bird flying overhead at the Volvo PGA on the European Tour. A rather significant dollop of bird doo landed with a thud on the shoulder of Mark McNulty's caddy. "It sounded like a golf ball landing," McNulty said. "My caddy decided it was a lucky sign."

That, of course, says it all about the profession, a caddy getting dumped on and thanking his lucky stars for the opportunity.

13

HELPING HANDS

When Tiger Woods stormed Augusta National for the first time, as a nineteen-year-old amateur, he brought with him Team Tiger, a concept created by his father, Earl. As an amateur, Tiger seldom played an important round without a team meeting. Earl was president of the team, Butch Harmon the coach. Jay Brunza was the team doctor, a psychologist, and also Woods's caddy. Kultida Woods was the team mother.

The grown-ups in professional golf snickered at the concept then, but the fact is that professional golf has evolved into a team game, albeit with only one player per team. Every professional golfer has a coach or a teacher. Many have sports psychologists. Some have personal trainers.

The olds pros Jackie Burke and Jimmy Demaret had their Jack Daniel's, the preeminent sports psychologist, to talk them off the ledge after a hard day at the office. The notion that golfers would consult a real psychologist would have met with derision in their day.

"Years ago, guys would have looked at you and said, 'What, are you kidding me?'" Jack Nicklaus said. "It's like when I was the first guy to do yardage books on the course. Guys looked at me and thought I was crazy. Do you know anybody who doesn't use yardage guides today? It's the same thing with sports psychologists."

Sports psychologists are prevalent today and are not relegated to background roles. Several have written books, most notable among them Dr. Bob Rotella and Dr. Richard Coop. Typically they will consult with clients by phone, though they often travel to tournament sites and are always on hand at major championships.

Payne Stewart even had a contract with Coop calling for Coop to stay with him during each of the four major championships, and requiring that Coop's other clients communicate with him by telephone if they wished to consult with him at night.

Davis Love III won the Tournament of Champions in 1993 with a cross-country assist from Rotella, who was home in Virginia. Love was leading by one stroke after three rounds, and inclement weather threatened to end the tournament prematurely, which would have made Love the winner by default.

"Everyone was saying that that was the end," Love said of Saturday's round. "I was trying not to believe them. I looked out the window a lot last night and this morning. My wife kept saying, 'It's going to rain, it's going to rain.' I said, 'Don't say that.' I didn't want to think that way."

He was unable to resist, however. On Sunday morning, he was in his room wrestling with the idea that they wouldn't play. Then the phone rang. It was Rotella, who somehow was sensing that his client's mind-set was not right and that it might prove costly if the final round was not canceled.

"Plan on playing," Rotella told him. "Get it in your head that you're going to play."

Love heeded the doctor's simple advice, shot a three-under-par 69 in conditions that weren't conducive to any kind of golf, much less high-quality golf, and won by a stroke.

"Rotella's call was very important," Love said. "I think that's how smart he is. He probably figured out how unsure I was of what was going on."

Rotella is among the busiest and most respected sports psychologists on the PGA Tour. He also has worked with the Georgia Tech golf team, where Stewart Cink became acquainted with him. On the morning before the Canon Greater Hartford Open began in 1997, Cink had breakfast with Rotella, a ninety-minute session.

"We were trying to dig into my psyche, trying to figure out what I was thinking when I had been playing so well," Cink said. "Basically what it came down to was concentrating on one shot at a time."

Cink's wife, Lisa, had told him precisely the same thing a few weeks earlier. It was her observation that he had been thinking in the future, rather than the present, an invitation for failure for the golfer. Rotella concurred with Lisa's diagnosis.

"It sounds like you might be paying a little too much attention to the leader boards and not taking it one shot at a time," Rotella told him.

"He reaffirmed the fact that I need to be staying in the present, one shot at a time, stick to my game plan, and don't try to do anything I can't do," Cink said.

The upshot? By Sunday afternoon, Cink, at 24, was a winner for the first time on the PGA Tour.

Billy Mayfair, a Rotella disciple, worked with the psychologist each night of the Tour Championship at Southern Hills in 1995. He was attempting to extinguish the demon thoughts that had crept into his psyche and had already cost him one tournament that year. Several weeks earlier, Mayfair had taken a three-stroke lead into the final nine holes of the World Series of Golf, when his mind began to betray him. He had worried that somehow he would lose a tournament that was his to win, a prophecy that eventually fulfilled itself. He bogeyed three straight holes on the back nine and wound up losing to Greg Norman in a playoff. "I had the tournament in my hands," Mayfair said, "and I lost it."

At Southern Hills he again took a three-stroke lead into the final round, when the negative thoughts arrived on schedule. Rotella's tack was to ask Mayfair whether anyone in the field would be so foolish as to decline an opportunity to trade positions with him. Of course not.

"Well, then," Rotella said, "let's be glad you have that three-stroke lead. And let's be totally prepared to win tomorrow."

Mayfair took these words of wisdom to heart and won the tournament, earning $540,000, the largest single payday of his career.

Three years later, Mayfair was tied for the lead at the Buick Open through fifty-four holes. On the morning of the final round, Mayfair had a telephone session with Rotella. The good doctor told him there was no pressure on him, that he already had won a tournament earlier that year, the Nissan Open.

"Just go out and have fun and enjoy yourself," Rotella told him.

Simple advice sometimes pays huge dividends. Mayfair birdied the first two holes to take the lead, which he held the remainder of the round for a two-stroke victory worth $324,000.

Sports psychologists make (club)house calls at major championships. Phil Mickelson was seen consulting with Rotella during the U.S. Open at Pinehurst in 1999, though he was not reclining on a couch.

"I enjoy being able to bounce some ideas off him and listen to some of his ideas," Mickelson said. "He's an intelligent guy that I have an opportunity to have conversations with and to learn from. It's a nice sounding board. It's been very beneficial in the sense that we've talked about how to regain confidence, or how to be patient on a tough golf course like those at the Masters or U.S. Open. It's very easy to get frustrated while trying to attack and make birdies."

Players also consult with swing doctors, as Mickelson attempted to do at the Open. He was trying to reach Burke, the former Masters and PGA Championship winner, at his Houston home to review areas on which they had been working together. "I tried calling him right after the round but couldn't quite get ahold of him," Mickelson said. "But I looked over some notes that I had taken from some of the things that he had said and went out to the range, and it's starting to feel a little bit better."

Players frequently turn to other players for advice. Brad Faxon once sought Jack Nicklaus's counsel. Faxon won a tournament one week, then tied for forty-eighth the following week. "I really need to learn how to play well after playing well, Jack," Faxon said.

"Jack nodded and I thought he'd tell me something really profound or magnificent, so I was really waiting for his answer, and he says, 'Join the club.'"

Faxon is among the game's best putters, and his counsel is frequently sought on the subject of putting. "Very few people come up to me on the range and ask me what I'm working on or thinking about," he said. "I get asked for putting lessons, though there's something about putting that's not as manly as hitting balls, like you're lucky to be a good putter."

Ted Tryba was on the putting green prior to the final round of the FedEx St. Jude Classic, when he was accosted by his friend Fulton Allem. "He kind of grabbed me and went, 'Look at me, cousin. You must take your time out there.' He told me to just take my time. Any time I felt a little rushed or uncomfortable I'd just take a step back and take my time."

His was a leisurely stroll to the winner's circle later that day to collect his second PGA Tour victory.

Steve Jones received an assist from a curious source at the start of the final round of the U.S. Open at Oakland Hills in 1996. Jones was paired with Tom Lehman, two devout Christians vying for one of the most prestigious prizes in golf. Lehman was reciting Bible scripture to help the man who threatened to take the U.S. Open trophy from him.

"You know," Lehman said to Jones on the first hole, "the Lord wants us to be courageous and strong, for that is the will of God."

Lehman repeated the advice as the pair made its way down the sixteenth fairway, with the outcome still in doubt. "I was really, really nervous," Jones said. "Tom said the same thing to me again and it really helped calm me."

Jones won the U.S. Open on the last hole, when Lehman's drive took a wickedly bad hop into a fairway bunker, leading to a bogey.

Lehman sought his own counsel a month later, prior to winning his lone major championship, the British Open at Royal Lytham and St. Anne's. After the third round, he encountered Nicklaus, who understands how to close a major championship. Lehman asked him for some advice.

"What do you need advice for?" Nicklaus said. "You have the game. You're solid."

Physical fitness is sweeping the PGA Tour and at least one man, Gabriel Hjertstedt, has a personal trainer with him. Trainer Boris Kuzmic was with Hjertstedt at the Tucson Open. On the practice tee before the final round Kuzmic gave his charge a pep talk that apparently worked. Hjertstedt won the tournament, his second PGA Tour victory.

Tiger Woods nearly withdrew from the Western Open in 1998, the victim of a spasm in his right hip early in the first round. "The plane was gassed up and ready to roll," his father, Earl, said. Woods, however, phoned a Las Vegas physical therapist with whom he works, Keith Klevin, who by telephone instructed Woods on drills that he might do to alleviate the pain.

"By the time I got to the golf course, I knew I was going to play," Woods said. "I felt fine by then. It was touch-and-go for a while."

Woods, who opened the tournament with a 76, rallied with rounds of 67, 69, and 69, to tie for ninth.

Though the concept of Team Tiger has diminished, Woods is not above seeking advice. He is among those who have sought wisdom on the art of putting from Faxon, asking him for a lesson at the JC Penney Classic one year.

"Yeah, you need a putting lesson," Faxon said. "You're only beating everyone by twenty shots. So what's your problem?"

"I can't seem to make them until the back nine on Sunday," Tiger said.

"Well, let me get to work on that for you," Faxon replied.

14

CANDID CAMERAS

The camera is everywhere now, even those places to which you'd rather it not go. ABC's executive producer Jack Graham recalled the player picking his nose at an inopportune time, with the camera up close and too personal, not to mention live.

The camera does not lie. At the JC Penney Classic, Steve Pate, nicknamed Volcano, split a tee marker in two by slamming his driver into it, the upshot of an errant tee shot. ESPN was there to air it live, golf's Mount Vesuvius blowing for the world to see. Pate's response? What could he say? "I hit my tee shot into a bunker," he said. "I didn't care for it at the time."

Every round of every PGA Tour event is now televised, requiring that players police their behavior in the event someone is watching. Or listening. Epithets in response to an errant shot occasionally are uttered within range of a boom microphone.

A timely epithet can alter perceptions. Fred Couples had been a frequent target of those who saw extraordinary talent but an apparent lack of passion and concluded that he did not care. Among them was Tom Weiskopf, who said that Couples had no goals and implied that his indifference and failure to fulfill others' expectations of him was somehow disgraceful. Couples's response? "His career has been a waste product, too."

It was not a spirited defense by Couples. A few years later, though, he inadvertently demonstrated that he indeed does care. In a playoff with Phil Mickelson at the Mercedes Championship at La Costa, Couples hit a drive off the tenth tee that took a wickedly bad hop, his ball winding up in a horrible position in a fairway bunker. When Couples arrived at the bunker and saw his predicament, he couldn't help himself. "Nice fucking deal," he said emphatically. Unfortunately, a boom mike was nearby, and his analysis came in loud and clear over live national television.

The term *angry golfer* is redundant, of course; all golfers are angry in the course of a round. Epithets in professional golf usually are muttered, but occasionally the player cannot help himself. Even Tiger Woods is not likely to complete a round without an outburst of some sort. On the seventeenth hole of the final round of the Mercedes Championship, for instance, he let fly a "Jesus Christ," a curious choice given his Buddhist leanings.

At the Kemper Open one year, a player was heard, too loud and clear, employing one of his pet phrases for a golf ball showing no inclination toward slowing down. "Grow teeth, motherfucker!" he said, treating a national television audience to PGA Tour jargon.

Players have a love-hate relationship with television. They love to appear on camera but hate having their play occasionally criticized by a broadcaster. The worst offender, from their viewpoint, is NBC's Johnny Miller, a refreshingly honest commentator who has never shied away from pointing out their foibles. Viewers, of course, don't share the players' perception of Miller; they welcome his honesty.

In Miller's first telecast for NBC, the Bob Hope Chrysler Classic in 1990, the network showed Chicago Bears coach Mike Ditka putting, then cut to a clip of him ranting on the sideline of a football game. "Looks like Curtis Strange after a three-putt," Miller said, setting the tone for his broadcast career and angering Strange in the process.

On the final hole on Sunday, as Peter Jacobsen stood over a 3-iron second shot over water to the eighteenth green at the Palmer Course at PGA West, Miller said, "This is absolutely the easiest shot to choke on that I've ever seen in my life."

Jacobsen executed the shot flawlessly, setting up his first victory in six years. Miller, meanwhile, set the tone for his television career by invoking the forbidden word, *choke*, for the first time, and certainly not the last time. He once even used the word in a positive manner. When the corpulent Tim Herron was in the process of winning the Honda Classic, Miller noted that "fat guys don't choke."

In the years to come, Miller frequently discussed choking and various other subjects to which the players generally objected. A faction of them concluded that the camera was candid enough, that it did not need commentary to further illuminate a player's flaws. Some wanted Miller banned from the locker room, though he seldom ventured there.

Miller provoked the players to anger again at the Ryder Cup in 1999. Justin Leonard played poorly the first two days, prompting Miller to say, "Justin needs to go back home and watch on TV. He has nothing going for him."

The players don't necessarily listen, but they hear. Leonard learned about Miller's comments and did not appreciate them. A day later, Leonard staged a remarkable comeback against Jose Maria Olazabal that culminated with a forty-five-foot putt at the seventeenth green that virtually cinched the Ryder Cup victory for the U.S. When NBC's Roger Maltbie began to query him on his match, Leonard replied with a shot at Miller: "I'm glad I didn't go home."

Players want to be shown in a good light, surely, but a segment of them also just want to be shown, in any light. Some actually have expressed concern about their lack of airtime—thinking, perhaps, not so much of their own egos as of the sponsors they wish to appease. When Mark O'Meara finished fourth in the Masters in 1992, he received zero airtime on Sunday's telecast, which meant that his visor with the Toyota logo across its front failed to appear.

The Toyota officials "were very upset and they've got every right to be," O'Meara said, without explaining where it says that a tournament underwritten by one car company, Cadillac, is required to provide free advertising to a competitor.

"I had friends say, 'Who'd you make mad at CBS?' I mean, I'm doing well coming in [to the final round]. At least give me a charity shot."

A year earlier, at the Bob Hope Chrysler Classic, O'Meara's Toyota visor received extensive television time, which reportedly incensed the tournament's sponsor. Chrysler's chairman, Lee Iacocca, was said to have complained to NBC. Incidentally, O'Meara's photograph appeared in the official program for the 1992 Bob Hope Chrysler Classic, and *Toyota* had been airbrushed from his visor.

It all gets very confusing, of course. Tiger Woods signed a lucrative endorsement contract with Buick, then in his first PGA Tour event with the Buick logo on his bag won the Mercedes Championship and a new Mercedes. For his fortieth birthday, O'Meara's wife presented him with a new Porsche, his endorsement contract with Toyota notwithstanding. A few weeks later he won the Buick Invitational. His record also includes victories in the Walt Disney World Oldsmobile Classic, the Honda Classic, the Mercedes Championship, and the Izusu-Kapalua International.

When he won the Buick Invitational, O'Meara was sensitive to the sponsor and had the presence of mind to toss his Toyota visor to his caddy, Jerry Higginbotham. He was savvy enough to know that Buick might frown on having its champion appear at post-tournament functions wearing a competitor's name.

Some players have been known to complain to the PGA Tour over their lack of airtime. A common objection is that the networks seemed to have turned their broadcasts, even on Thursdays and Fridays, into a Tiger Woods documentary by focusing on Woods to the exclusion of others.

It is a peculiar argument, since Tigermania is largely responsible for the substantial increases in tournament purses. People want to watch the stars. Even if Tiger seems to be out of contention, it is not prudent to focus the camera elsewhere, as he demonstrated at the Phoenix Open in 1997, when he made a hole in one at the sixteenth hole.

"My opinion is that they're missing the boat," ABC's Graham said. "Everyone should thank their lucky stars Tiger's out here. They should be kissing his ring every day. It bears out in the ratings, too. They've doubled and tripled. We're trying to keep the viewers watching."

Scott Hoch is the most outspoken player on the subject of airtime, or lack of it. "I probably don't get the respect I deserve," Hoch said in a *Golf Digest* dialogue, "but then I look at my record and see a double-edged sword: I've been a very consistent player, but not a great player. I've been close to greatness a number of times, but haven't achieved it. So I can see why people say that, and why I don't get much respect from the press or TV.

"Actually, my problem with TV comes from the amount of airtime I've received. You can tell how much you're respected by how much they show you on TV. I just don't get much television time compared with other people well below me, in career accomplishments or even what they have done that year."

Hoch tied for fifth in the Masters in 1996, the year in which Greg Norman took a six-stroke lead into the final round and wound up five shots in arrears of the champion, Nick Faldo. "On Sunday it was the Faldo and Norman show," Hoch said. "They didn't show anybody else."

Why would they? No other players had a role in this unfolding drama that was akin to watching a train wreck. Much as people tried, they could not turn away.

"People believe whatever they see and hear on TV," Hoch said. "If they don't show you very much on TV, or if you do well and they don't make much notice about it, then the people watching don't really notice what you're doing."

Airtime can be determined by a director's perception of a particular player. Chris Perry, for instance, has been known to start and stop so often that directors aren't certain whether he actually intends to pull the trigger. It bothers some to the extent that they are disinclined to show him at all unless his presence at or near the top of the leader board demands it.

A player's nuances also are factored into a telecast. Lanny Wadkins, for instance, plays so fast that "a guy's ball hasn't stopped rolling yet and Lanny already has hit his shot," Graham said. Accordingly, he is prepared to react quickly. Conversely, "Justin Leonard always gets over a putt and backs off," Graham said. "So you know you don't have to rush to that hole. It helps to know their idiosyncrasies."

There are those occasions when players wished that they hadn't appeared on television. The role television plays in golf has on occasion been an intrusive one, costing players money and possibly altering the tournament outcome, by becoming an interactive affair.

The most famous incident involved Craig Stadler, whose drive on the twelfth hole in the third round of the Andy Williams Open at Torrey Pines stopped beneath a tree, requiring that he kneel to hit the shot. An overnight thunderstorm had saturated the ground, and to keep his trousers from getting wet, Stadler put a towel down and knelt on that.

On its Sunday telecast of the tournament, NBC aired highlights from Saturday's round, one of them involving Stadler kneeling on a towel to hit a shot. At that point, the phones in the PGA Tour office began ringing, viewers calling to inform officials that Stadler had violated a rule.

Indeed, rule 13–3 in the *Rules of Golf* preclude a player from building a stance, and the manner in which Stadler had done so was even covered in the United States Golf Association's book on interpretation of rules, *Decisions of Golf.*

Glenn Tait, a PGA Tour official, went to NBC's production facility and reviewed the tape in question and concluded that Stadler had violated the rule, and because he had not assessed himself the requisite two-stroke penalty, he had signed an incorrect score, resulting in his disqualification. Compounding the error was the fact that Stadler closed the tournament with a 68 that would have tied him for second place, earning him $37,333. Instead, he earned nothing.

"I can't tell you all the philosophies of the *Decisions of Golf*," Tait said. "Some sound peculiar to you. Some are peculiar to us."

This was perhaps peculiar to all. Had Stadler simply donned his rain pants to hit the shot, no penalty. Asked about the difference between rain pants and a towel, Tait replied, "I don't see any difference."

Stadler declined to comment in the immediate aftermath of his disqualification, but later said he agreed with the ruling. A week later, meanwhile, a fan shouted to him, "You should have just taken your pants off!"

"That would be pretty, wouldn't it?" Stadler replied. "I wouldn't want to make anybody sick."

A few years later, Paul Azinger was the victim of an overzealous viewer in Colorado. In the second round of the Doral Open in Miami, Azinger was standing within a water hazard to hit a shot and, in an attempt to improve his footing, inadvertently dislodged a rock. The following morning, the viewer in Colorado phoned PGA Tour officials and informed them of the violation, which carries a two-stroke penalty. Tour officials reviewed the videotape and concluded that the viewer was correct. When Azinger came off the course after completing the third round, he was informed that he had been disqualified for having signed an incorrect scorecard the day before.

"That's not quite right," Mark Calcavecchia said. "It shouldn't be up to some guy in Colorado. It should be up to our officials and the two guys playing with him."

Azinger also was penalized two strokes at the Tournament of Champions when a horrific 8-iron shot put his ball on the lip of a green-side bunker. He took his time assessing the shot, at one point reaching down and absentmindedly removing a leaf about six inches away. He began his pre-shot routine again, and the ball suddenly rolled back into a bunker.

A PGA Tour official ruled that Azinger had not yet addressed his ball and that he was entitled to play it from the bunker. A viewer, meanwhile, phoned the PGA Tour and informed officials that Azinger's ball had moved *after* he had removed a loose impediment within one club length, a violation of the rules.

Tait intercepted Azinger coming off the eighteenth green and asked that he not sign his card until they reviewed the videotape. When Azinger saw the tape, he agreed that a two-stroke penalty was a correct ruling.

Viewers aren't always right. At the U.S. Open at Pinehurst, Hoch was required to mark his ball in a bunker. After doing so, he handed his ball to his caddy, Greg Rita. A viewer phoned Pinehurst and claimed that Rita had cleaned the ball. Had he done so, the rules would have required a one-stroke penalty. An official investigated the matter but threw out the case, citing a lack of evidence.

Lee Janzen was disqualified from the World Series of Golf, courtesy of television viewers. A birdie putt hovered on the lip, seemingly uncertain whether to stay or fall. Janzen bent to examine the ball, as did his playing partner, Vijay Singh. Twenty seconds passed, and Janzen concluded that it would not fall. As he prepared to tap it in, the ball indeed dropped.

Janzen later signed for a 3. However, several television viewers phoned in and notified tour officials that Janzen had violated Rule

16-2, which limits the waiting time to ten seconds. PGA Tour officials assessed a one-stroke penalty, which meant that Janzen had signed an incorrect scorecard, ending his tournament after one round.

A valid argument is that had the same violations been committed by those who were not in contention and as a result did not appear on television, no one would have known and no penalties would have been assessed.

Television might have influenced the outcome of the PGA Championship at Valhalla in 1996. When Kenny Perry had finished his final round in the lead, CBS invited him into the booth for an interview. This is not unusual, though typically the interview lasts only a few minutes and the player departs. Those who have completed their rounds and face the possibility of a playoff almost always repair to the practice tee to keep loose. Perry chose to linger in the booth, however. When Mark Brooks birdied the eighteenth hole, Perry found himself in a playoff, for which he was not prepared, not having hit a ball for forty-five minutes.

"I asked them [the officials], 'Do I have time to go and hit some balls?'" Perry said. "And they first said, 'Yes.' I took off for the range, and then they grabbed me and said, 'No, you can't.' I was probably caught up in the moment with all the people. I learned a good lesson, I guess. It's a hard one."

Perry was defeated by Brooks in the playoff. He had spent forty minutes in the tower, but CBS was unapologetic. "It was his option [to stay]," Jim Nantz said. Perry acknowledged that it might have been his undoing. "Maybe I let my mind wander," he said.

Those who aren't used to the camera's attention also are susceptible to allowing their minds to wander. Joe Durant played well enough in the first round of the U.S. Open at the Olympic Club to attract television attention, a disruptive influence.

"I started getting a little nervous," he said. "The crowd started getting a little bigger and a lot more cameras were out there following us, so at that point I started feeling it a little bit."

Mark Carnevale confessed to thoughts of television cameras when he played himself into contention in the first round of the U.S. Open at the Olympic Club. He then skulled an 8-iron, which brought him back to reality and returned his focus to the task at hand.

The post-round television interview can be a dicey affair. When Tim Herron was a PGA Tour rookie and virtually unknown, he took a six-stroke lead after thirty-six holes of the Honda Classic. A local television reporter requested an interview, and Herron obliged him. The first question: "Who *are* you?"

Nick Faldo closed the PGA Championship with a second consecutive round of 75, perhaps doing irreparable harm to his chances of becoming a captain's pick for the European Ryder Cup team.

"Well," said a BBC broadcaster, "a score of 75 hasn't done much for your Ryder Cup cause, has it?"

"You're so fucking negative," Faldo replied before storming off.

Television occasionally comes to a player's rescue, too. CBS commentator Gary McCord noticed that Steve Pate apparently was going to tee off in the Atlanta Classic wearing light pants bearing a noticeable chili stain near his crotch, the remnants of a spicy, sloppy breakfast.

McCord volunteered to trade pants with Pate, who accepted his offer.

15

DAY OF RECKONING

The word is a loathsome one of five letters that, on an obscenity scale, trumps even the variety of four-letter words that players routinely inject into their vocabulary. The word surfaces only on Sunday, the day of reckoning in tournament week, the day on which careers and reputations turn, the day on which those with doubts hope only that they don't *choke*.

There it is, the vilest word in golf, one that players find so repugnant that they are loath even to permit it to cross their lips, as though doing so might pass as an invitation for it to seize their psyche. Evidence in support of this theory exists. John Huston was near the lead early in the Mercedes Championship in 1995, earning him an invitation to the media room for an interview. Sitting on the dais, he took a drink from his water bottle, swallowed improperly, and began coughing. "I think I'm going to choke," he said, eliciting laughter from the press corps. In the final round, Huston let a four-stroke lead slip away, and he eventually lost the tournament.

Ken Venturi once shot a final-round 80 to lose the Masters by a single stroke, yet he refused to say that he had choked. "I prefer to call it 'unfamiliarity with the situation,'" he said.

Tom Kite once told his teacher Harvey Penick that he had started to choke down on his putter. Penick winced. "Tommy, don't use that word," Penick told him. "Don't think of choking down on your putter. Think of gripping down on your putter."

Scott Hoch hates the word, too. Hoch, to his dismay, rhymes with choke, as *Sports Illustrated* once uncharitably pointed out in a headline. Hoch had only to navigate a simple two and a half feet in a playoff to win the Masters, though simplicity in this game is a sliding scale. Two and a half feet is a gimme on Saturday at home, but it is a treacherous undertaking on Sunday at Augusta, on slick greens, with the Masters at stake. Hoch's putt slid by, and Nick Faldo eventually won the green jacket.

Hoch's career should not be defined by what he failed to accomplish, inasmuch as he has won eight PGA Tour events and has been one of the consistently better players of his generation. Just as he's lost tournaments on the final hole, he has won them, too. At the Milwaukee Open in 1997, he holed a sixty-foot eagle chip on the final hole to win it. "The squirrel found an acorn," he said, hinting at his mind-set with tournaments on the line. He said he was thankful he did not leave the chip four feet from the hole. "It might have been a different story," he said.

Sundays are where dreams go to die on the PGA Tour. Nerves jangle and stomachs churn, and the clubs over which players had control the previous three days stage juntas and declare their independence.

Arnold Palmer won his last major championship in 1964, though he won seventeen PGA Tour events after that. Still, the pressure began to unnerve him, particularly in majors. "I admitted to several close confidants," he wrote in his book, A *Golfer's Life*, "beginning in about 1965, every time I'd get close to a major prize, my hands would begin to shake, and for a moment or two, when it counted most, the demons of doubt would whisper in my ear and I honestly wondered if I could win again."

In the U.S. Open in 1966, Palmer held a seven-stroke lead with nine holes to play, only to dribble it away, then lost to Billy Casper in a playoff the following day. "I had totally negative thoughts on every swing," he said. "I just couldn't swing."

Casper was more succinct, concluding that Palmer panicked. "I had never seen him panic before," Casper said. "He just panicked when I started catching up."

Tension does not discriminate among those in contention. Palmer once bogeyed six straight holes on the back nine of the final round of a Senior PGA Tour event, gift-wrapping a victory for Don January in the process. In the clubhouse lounge later, he was sitting with the baseball legend Stan Musial, when a phone next to them began ringing. Musial answered it, and Palmer listened to one side of the conversation.

"Uh, no, actually, Palmer didn't win," Musial told the caller.

"What happened?" Musial said, repeating the caller's question. Musial began stammering, afraid to reveal the truth with the victim seated next to him. Sensing his discomfort, Palmer grabbed the phone from Musial and shouted into the mouthpiece.

"He choked his ass off!"

So it goes on any given Sunday on the PGA Tour, when pressure unilaterally enforces its authority without regard to a player's résumé. A golfer's ability to play through it determines the degree to which he succeeds or fails. "Everybody chokes," said J. L. Lewis, who won the John Deere Classic in 1999. "It's just a matter of what are you going to do about it, you know? After you've wasted something, you just have to forget about it and go on."

Hoch bristled when *Sports Illustrated* injected rhyme into the reason that he failed to win the Masters. Yet at the Houston Open in 1995, Hoch held a seven-stroke lead with thirteen holes to play and was still five shots ahead with seven holes to play. At that point, his swing began to go awry, and he was required to hole a thirty-five-foot putt for birdie just to get into a playoff. He'd lost his grip on a lead that should have been insurmountable and wound up losing to Payne Stewart in a playoff.

"You can print it now," Hoch said. "That's why Hoch rhymes with choke. It was just pitiful. You can write whatever you want. It's probably less than I feel. It's just a joke."

Stewart was a grateful recipient of the victory, though he preferred not to have heard that Hoch used that abominable word.

"I hate that word," he said. "I'm sorry to hear he used it. It's a nasty, nasty word. But who am I to argue?"

Stewart, who eventually won the U.S. Open twice, let another Open slip away at Shinnecock Hills in 1986. A late bogey erased his lead and coincided with a long par putt holed by Raymond Floyd. Stewart acknowledged that he was unable to handle the pressure represented by the stakes, a U.S. Open championship, and the man with whom he was vying, the seemingly indomitable Floyd. Still, Stewart declined to admit that he choked, confessing only to a failure to "close the sale."

No sale was the fate of Greg Norman's attempt to peddle the notion that something other than his inability to handle the pressure was responsible for his astonishing collapse at the Masters in 1996. A six-stroke lead on Saturday became a five-stroke loss on Sunday and begged to be attributed to the forbidden word, though few would give it voice, as if doing so would constitute piling on.

The fraternity of Masters winners is among the most exclusive in golf, and few covet the green jacket as passionately as Greg Norman. He opened the Masters that year with a 63 and by Saturday night had a six-stroke lead that was the equivalent of having slipped on the first sleeve of the green jacket. In the process, the Masters went from a tournament that was his to win to one that was his to lose, golf's version of the preventive defense.

Perhaps no one in the history of golf has been snakebitten as often as Norman, who lost the PGA Championship when Bob Tway holed a sand shot on the final hole in 1986; who was felled by an improbable chip holed by Larry Mize in a Masters playoff in 1987; who lost the Nestle Invitational when Robert Gamez holed his second shot for eagle at the last hole in 1990; who lost the USF&G Classic when David Frost holed a sand shot at the last hole in 1990.

This time he was the culprit as well as the victim, his own worst enemy. In a five-hole stretch on Sunday, Norman lost six shots to Nick Faldo. Amen Corner, eleven through thirteen at Augusta National, defended its reputation at Norman's expense. Brandel Chamblee, who used to ride cutting horses, was asked how doing so compared with playing Amen Corner. "It's very similar when you get your foot caught in the saddle and you fall off," he said. "It's the same sort of feeling." Norman understood the feeling. He bogeyed and double-bogeyed the first two-thirds of Amen Corner, dropping himself into second place. By day's end, he was on the wrong side of an eleven-stroke turnaround, shooting 78, while Faldo shot 67 to win the green jacket for the third time.

"What do you say?" Norman's friend Nick Price said. "There's nothing you can say to him. I think everybody's nauseous."

Even Faldo was at a loss for words. "I told him I didn't know what to say, that I just wanted to give him a hug," Faldo said. "I honestly, genuinely felt sorry for him. What he's gone through has been horrible."

Norman knew what to say: "I played like shit." What he did not say was that he choked. Others struggled to avoid saying it—a difficult task, since the evidence was overwhelming. The *Kansas City Star* was among those who had no problem delivering a guilty verdict. It ran a list it entitled "Other Choke Artists," including Marcia Clark, Chris Darden, H.J. Heimlich, and the Boston Strangler.

"They don't understand," Norman said in response to those who claimed that he choked. "People always want to take the sensational side. You watch television nowadays and it's all the harshness and sensational and negative. These people don't have a clue."

Surely what they can't possibly have a clue about is what it's like to play professional tournament golf and be in contention on Sunday.

"Sunday golf on the PGA Tour, it's a menagerie of emotions,

different scenarios and different things that go on," Steve Elkington said. "It's so hard to win. People don't understand how hard it is to execute under that type of pressure."

The short putts so easy early in the week are stretched by the pressure of the moment, the hole shrinking rapidly. "My fingers start jumping, the nerve ends are popping, and I can't breath," Curtis Strange said, attempting to describe the feeling. "One of the most important things I have to remember to do is breathe."

This is not atypical of players in contention on Sunday. Andrew Magee was asked how he handles pressure. "I just try and breathe," he said.

Notah Begay III, a PGA Tour rookie who already had won once on tour, nonetheless found himself increasingly uncomfortable as the pressure increased late in the final round at the Michelob Championship in 1999. "I told my caddy on the second hole in the playoff that I felt like I was suffocating with the rain and the cloud cover and the situation," Begay said. "I wasn't choking. I just felt like I had a lot of nervous energy. I was just trying to calm myself down. There's really no way to overcome it. You just go right through it. It's like driving through smoke. You know what's on the other side, and you have to go through it and trust yourself, that you're going to steer straight."

David Ogrin once offered smiling as a respiratory stimulus. "When you smile," he said, "you breathe." He also said that many golf tournaments are lost from "a lack of endorphins." He smiled frequently and apparently had a full supply of endorphins when he won the La Cantera Texas Open, fending off a fourth-round challenge by a tour rookie, Tiger Woods, in 1996.

On a U.S. Open telecast of the third round, Johnny Miller spoke of the difficulty of breathing under pressure. "Today the guys are breathing Q-tips," he said. "Tomorrow they'll be breathing cotton balls."

Even Hale Irwin, a three-time U.S. Open champion, was susceptible to breathing difficulties under pressure on Sunday, albeit with the Ryder Cup on the line. "I couldn't breathe," he said. "I couldn't swallow. The sphincter factor was high."

Attempting to win for the first time increases pressure and difficulty exponentially. Even Tiger Woods required professional refinement of the killer instinct he had developed as an amateur. Only twenty, he took a third-round lead into the Quad City Classic in 1996, his third event as a professional. His father, Earl, boasted that Woods had never lost an event that he was leading entering the final round, and he expected form to prevail here.

Yet on the fourth hole, Woods attempted to fade his tee shot but pull-hooked it into a pond instead. He took a drop and attempted to hit a difficult recovery shot, threading the needle through some trees. His ball caromed off a tree and back into the pond. Eventually, he concluded the hole in eight strokes, a quadruple bogey that turned a three-stroke advantage into a one-stroke deficit. Woods tied for fifth. By his fifth event as a pro, Woods was a winner and the golf world would never be the same. Still, he had to endure a learning curve.

Those who have yet to obtain financial security also have the potential windfall with which to concern themselves. "The tour," Phil Blackmar once said, "is like having a chance to win the lottery every week, and there are only one hundred fifty-six tickets."

Bill Glasson recalled his state of mind when he was en route to his first PGA Tour victory in the Kemper Open in 1985. "I wasn't trying to win my first tournament," he said, "I was trying not to have a heart attack before I finished the seventy-second hole. On the seventeenth hole, I turned around to say something to my caddy and nothing came out. I mean, it wasn't a matter of winning. It was a matter of just trying to finish without bleeding to death."

A tour rookie, Rich Beem, found himself in a position to win the Kemper Open in 1999, which threatened to make him physically ill. "I was lying in bed and I honestly felt like I was going to throw up," he said. Beem bought a bottle of Pepto-Bismol to settle his stomach, though he concealed it from the other players. "Hid it in my pocket so nobody would see," he said. "I carried it into the locker room and went to the bathroom. I went into a stall, took a couple of big chugs. That kind of calmed me a little bit."

For a couple of hours, anyway. At the thirteenth tee, even a four-stroke lead failed to provide him with comfort. "Get me through this," he said to his caddy, Steve Duplantis.

Beem spotted a few reporters following his quest. "I'm wiped out, man," he said.

He noted afterward that in those situations "par is your friend," and somehow he managed to befriend four of them in a row, which made an eighteenth-hole bogey immaterial. He won by a stroke.

J.L. Lewis won his first PGA Tour event in stifling heat that still was not as uncomfortable as the heat generated by the pressure of the moment. "The heat from the situation was much more difficult," he said. "There's a lot of pressure on you to win out here. Everything is based on winning. Nobody cares about anything else, really."

Joe Durant missed the eighteenth green with his second shot in the final round of the Motorola Western Open, then muffed his third, hitting it maybe five feet. "I panicked," he said. Still, he managed to make bogey, giving him a two-stroke victory.

Kevin Sutherland did not shy away from the dreaded word when he backpedaled one Sunday. He began the final round of the Canon Greater Hartford Open one stroke behind the leader, D. A. Weibring, then shot 74 and finished eight strokes back.

"I was choking my guts out the last few holes," he said. "I wanted tap-ins on every green, and I didn't get them."

David Duval developed a reputation for final-round failures before he broke through with three consecutive victories at the end of the 1997 season on his way to assuming the No. 1 ranking in the world. Tied for the lead after three rounds of the BellSouth Classic in 1997, he closed with a 72 and lost by three. "If y'all want to call it choking, or if I want to call it choking, it doesn't bother me," Duval said.

Jeff Maggert was another consistently strong player who frequently tripped on his way to the winner's circle. His victory in the WGC–Andersen Consulting Match Play Championship earned him $1 million and was his first victory in six years. Needless to say, he was asked about nerves.

"Being nervous is good," he said. "If you expect to be nervous it's easier to handle. Guys who can play well when they're nervous are the guys that win tournaments. You can't be afraid of it. Everyone chokes in golf. That is just a fact of life. I have choked before."

Tour veterans will tell you that if you continually jockey into position to win, eventually it will happen in spite of the obstacles. "One thing I've learned about being in contention," Elkington said, "is that you don't have to go berserk out there to win. You just have to be there. At the end inevitably something happens. We all run out of holes."

Victory still has the capacity to sidestep those who frequently play themselves into contention. Bobby Wadkins is among them, playing twenty-five years on the PGA Tour without winning, a fact of which he is reminded more often that he'd like.

"Nothing would make me happier than to come in here [to the media room] and buy all you guys champagne so you could never write that again," Wadkins said.

The rub of the green felled him on a couple of occasions. He had a chance to win the Kemper Open one year, leading by a couple of shots, when he attempted to reach the par-5 sixteenth hole in two shots. "I knew if I made birdie or eagle, I'd have a five-shot lead," he said. He hung the shot to the right of the green and was unable to find the ball.

"You don't expect to lose a golf ball in a PGA Tour tournament with twenty thousand people watching you play."

The shot and lost ball cost him the tournament. He lost to Mark Brooks.

In 1979, Wadkins had a chance to win the IVB-Philadelphia Classic. He hit what seemed to be a perfect tee shot at the eighteenth hole, but the ball hit a sprinkler head on the fly, which sent it bounding into a bush, leaving him with an unplayable lie. He wound up in a playoff with Lou Graham, who birdied the first extra hole to win.

The plight of Mark Wiebe at the Kemper Open in 1997 was the kind of experience that leads players to consider exorcism. Seemingly a certain winner, Wiebe began missing short putts, including one at the eighteenth hole to lose the tournament.

"I'm speechless," he said. "I don't know what to say."

His demise began at the eighth hole, when he missed a four-foot par putt. "That's when I started my three-putting binge," he said. He missed a three-and-a-half-foot putt at nine, then recovered partially, by making longer birdie putts at ten and thirteen. At the seventeenth hole, the demons returned, and he missed a three-foot putt. "That's the only time I got a little shaky," he said. "I felt a little bit nervous."

At eighteen, he three-putted again, needing only to hole a putt that did not stretch to three feet to tie for the lead and move into a playoff. He missed.

"When you hit putts like that," he said, "it's not meant to be, I guess. I've been a little bit shaky on my smaller putts all week long. Even the ones I made, my hands felt a little quivery."

The beneficiary was Justin Leonard, whom Wiebe encountered by the eighteenth green. "I congratulated him," Wiebe said, though the two did not have an extended conversation. "I was kind of busy going to sign my card and he was kind of busy going to get the trophy."

It was not the first time this had happened to Wiebe, either, though it was the first time it had happened with a tournament on the line and a television audience bearing witness.

"It happened in Dallas, too," he said. "I missed a bunch of putts there and my hands were quivering and it shocked me, because I wasn't expecting it. It's not fun when you feel like your hands are shaking, and you're trying to win a tournament. I'm irked, but my putter got me in the position to win, so I can't really complain. My dad would say, 'You should have hit it closer.'"

Wiebe, in fact, began to grow concerned over those quivering hands. He was home in Denver, attempting to insert a Phillips head drill bit into a screw and his hands would not permit him to do so. "That scared me a lot," he said. Doctors identified it as intention tremors, eventually attributed to a chemical imbalance rather than to his having choked.

Headed to the practice tee at the Riviera Country Club prior to the final round of the Los Angeles Open one year, Fred Couples heard the forbidden word from someone in the crowd.

"Have a good day," the man said, "and don't choke."

Couples refused to let the comment pass. "I have a smart mouth myself," he said, "so I responded."

He responded again when he hit his tee shot at the first hole left of the fairway and out of bounds, erasing the one-stroke lead he had taken into the final round. Couples eventually regained his equilibrium and prevailed, holing a twelve-foot birdie putt on the second playoff hole to defeat Davis Love III.

Another forbidden word is *yips*, a nervous condition that causes the hands to twitch at impact when putting, particularly on short putts. Tom Watson calls these twitches "the flinches," a condition that he has had to overcome. Neither cause nor cure is known, but the yips are debilitating; they have ended careers. "If you can't putt," said Ben Crenshaw, one of the best putters in history, "you're in a lot of trouble out here. A lot of guys hit it super, but can't stick it in the hole. Arnold Palmer, for instance, and Ben Hogan and Sam Snead near the end of their careers. Maybe that seems unfair, but that's the way it is."

Johnny Miller fought the yips most of his career. He won the British Open in 1976 by painting a dot on the grip of his putter, a focal point for his eyes during the stroke. Once he lined up the putt, he never looked at the ball.

"Putting affects the nerves more than anything," Byron Nelson once said. "I would actually get nauseated over three-footers, and there were tournaments when I couldn't keep a meal down for four days."

"It's a crazy game, isn't it?" Scott Gump asked rhetorically.

He had just failed in his attempt to win for the first time and in the process derail the best player in the world at the time, David Duval, at the Players Championship in 1999. He was down one when he came to the infamous seventeenth hole at the TPC at Sawgrass, a par-3 with an island green. The pin was tucked in the back right corner of the green, precariously close to the water. Still, Gump needed to attempt to make birdie to win. A 9-iron, he figured, would not be enough club to get the ball back to the pin. He chose an 8-iron.

"I just choked down on it," he said, employing the word that made Harvey Penick wince, "really smoothed it. Unfortunately, I knew it as soon as I hit it, it was in the water. I was trying to hit just a little cut, and I killed it."

The ball landed on the green, then rolled off the back edge, into the water, killing his chances.

Len Mattiace also was victimized by the seventeenth at Sawgrass, when he too was attempting to win for the first time. He trailed Justin Leonard by a single shot. Mattiace's cancer-stricken mother Joyce was nearby, watching from her wheelchair. Mattiace stared down one of the most menacing tee shots in golf, then hit it over the green and into the water. His next shot found the front bunker. His skulled his fourth shot over the green and back into the water, leading to a score of 8. "My heart came out of my body," Mattiace said, "two or three times."

Ken Green experienced pressure of another sort. He went through a bitter divorce and custody battle and was ordered by a divorce judge to continue playing tournament golf at a time when he wanted to take a one-year hiatus to get his life back in order. "I'm out there panicking on the golf course, thinking, 'This shot is going to cost me this much money,'" he said. "You can't play golf that way."

Even before his domestic troubles, he was a victim of nerves. He once described how he choked in the third round of the International. "It was scary," he said, "like I was playing for my life. My knees were literally shaking. Topping a drive coming in, I told Shelly [his sister and caddy], 'This is unbelievable. My body's gone haywire.'"

Green recovered adequately to post his second PGA Tour victory the next day.

Players attempt to trick their mind into disregarding the pressure, as Olin Browne did at the Greater Harford Open in 1998. He had finished seventy-two holes and in all likelihood was headed to a playoff, though the man with whom he would vie was still on the course. Browne chose to wait out the suspense on the putting green with his kids, Olin and Alexandra, and a friend.

"I wasn't going to stress about it," he said. "The best way to deal with stress is take your mind off whatever is stressing you out. So we had a putting contest. My daughter and I beat Olin and Patrick. I tried to relax a little bit."

When he learned that indeed he was in a playoff, he eschewed the free ride in a cart and walked back to the eighteenth tee. "Everybody was hollering at me," he said. "I did that because I'd been sitting around for twenty minutes. I hadn't hit any balls. I felt it was a good way to loosen up and maybe pick up some good vibes on the way back."

A few minutes later, Browne holed a forty-foot chip shot to win for the first time on the PGA Tour.

The shots that can win or lose a major championship exert the worst kind of pressure, given their historical significance. Norman's Sunday collapse at Augusta solidified his as a career remembered more for the losses than the victories. Only a summer before, Corey Pavin stood in the fairway at the eighteenth hole of the U.S. Open at Shinnecock Hills, carrying the label *the best player never to have won a major,* and faced the most important shot of his career. He had two hundred nine yards to the front edge of the green, two twenty-eight to the hole, a 4-wood shot.

"It was just a matter of going through my routine," he said. "I took my time. I made sure I was absolutely ready to hit that shot. If I had to sit there for ten minutes, I was going to sit there for ten minutes. I was going to make sure that when I got over the ball I knew what I wanted to do and had all my swing thoughts in order. I aimed it at the right edge of the green, put it back in my stance, and when I saw it come off the club face, I knew I'd hit a good shot. It was probably the best shot I've ever hit under pressure."

As he walked toward the green, he said a little prayer. "I just wanted to let Him know that this was for Him, to glorify Him," Pavin said, "and I don't know what that meant because I missed the putt on eighteen. He wanted me to sweat a little bit more, I guess."

Pavin then went to the television booth and waited to see whether Greg Norman might catch him. Norman needed to hole his second shot from the fairway, which, predictably, he failed to do. Pavin was the U.S. Open champion.

Mike Reid was five strokes ahead of Payne Stewart in the PGA Championship at Kemper Lakes in 1989. Stewart staged a rally but remained two strokes behind when he completed play, with Reid still on the course, three holes from the finish line.

"The last nine holes of a major, some really strange things happen," said Stewart, who stood by waiting patiently to test his prescient theory.

Reid cooperated, surrendering five shots over the final three holes and the championship to Stewart. "It's only a game, right?" Reid said tearfully. "I cry at supermarket openings. Someday I'll do it right and finish one of these."

Indeed, at the Masters earlier in the year he led with six holes to play and finished sixth. After opening the PGA Championship with a 66, he was asked to reflect on the Masters. "I'd rather use the Masters as a stepping-stone than a tombstone," he said. "To be honest, I appreciated the chance to choke."

Jim Simons was still an amateur when he led the U.S. Open through three rounds and was seeking to become the first amateur to win the event since John Goodman won it in 1933. He was to be paired with Jack Nicklaus in the fourth and final round, an imposing task for a seasoned pro, and especially daunting for an amateur. Simons was rooming with his former Wake Forest teammate, Lanny Wadkins, that week. When they were preparing to leave for the course, Wadkins noticed something amiss with Simons's outfit.

"Jim," he said, "your shirt is on inside out."

"As I pulled the shirt over my head," Simons said, "I remember thinking, 'This might be a tough day.'"

It was. Simons shot a 76 and finished fifth, still a reputable showing for an amateur, but indicative of what some call the toughest day in golf, Sunday at the Open.

Mark Calcavecchia became a sympathetic figure at the Ryder Cup in 1991, when he was 4-up with four holes to play in his singles match with Colin Montgomerie. Calcavecchia triple-bogeyed the fifteenth to lose the hole and bogeyed the sixteenth to lose that hole. Yet when Montgomerie hit his tee shot into the water at the par-3 seventeenth, Calcavecchia seemingly was assured a victory and a critical point for the U.S. team. Instead, he skulled his tee shot so pitifully that it made it only halfway across the water. Moments later, he missed a two-foot putt, enabling Montgomerie to win another hole. Calcavecchia capped the match with another bogey at eighteen to lose that hole, resulting in a halve with Montgomerie.

It was among golf's most ignominious finishes, and Calcavecchia was inconsolable, even after the United States eventually prevailed over the European team.

"I've had enough tension this week to last a lifetime," said Calcavecchia, who was an accomplished player, even under the most difficult of circumstances, and only two years earlier had won the British Open.

Some thought he would never recover, that the power of negative thinking when pressure was dialed up would undo him. On the contrary, Calcavecchia went on to win another four PGA Tour events and three international events, including the Subaru Sarazen World Open in Braselton, Georgia, in 1997, where he set a course record, a 62. "I just kind of kept making twenty-footers every other hole," he said. "It was almost embarrassing, really, because the guys you're playing with are fixing to throw up."

He had won the BellSouth Classic on the PGA Tour a few years earlier, even though the demons reappeared and threatened to undermine him again. As he addressed his ball on one tee shot, he stepped away and asked whoever was jingling the change in his pocket to cease doing so. Later he acknowledged making it up. "I didn't know if my brain was rattling," he said.

Sunday golf will do that to golfers, even those who have succeeded in the face of such pressure, as Calcavecchia ultimately did in the BellSouth.

"Handling pressure is funny," Calcavecchia said afterward. "Sometimes you're able to do it, and sometimes you aren't. Today I was, and I'm not sure why. I know this puts [the Ryder Cup at] Kiawah Island further behind me. I've proved I can hit shots when I have to."

The former manager Gene Mauch possessed a brilliant baseball mind that was tested one day when he was asked how, when the pressure was peaking, notably in October, Reggie Jackson consistently responded successfully. Mauch stared pensively ahead as he contemplated the question. He concluded finally that under pressure others' ability to perform diminished. Jackson, he said, did not necessarily elevate his game; it only appeared so in view of the fact that he took advantage of a pitcher's mistakes brought on by the pressure.

Tiger Woods has dispelled this theory, by consistently raising his level of play in response to the pressure. He did so at the PGA Championship in 1999, holing a difficult downhill left-to-right putt to save par on the seventeenth hole. He did it again at the season-opening Mercedes Championship in 2000, playing the final three holes in eagle, birdie, and birdie, the last on a forty-foot putt that defeated Ernie Els in a playoff.

Confidence is the offensive lineman opening the hole that allows talent to come through. Woods obviously has an ample supply of confidence and talent. For the rest of the golf world, confidence tends to take periodic leaves of absence.

Brad Faxon was a veteran of thirteen years on the PGA Tour, though he had failed to win in more than four years, when he arrived at the eighteenth tee at English Turn with a four-stroke lead in the final round of the Freeport-McDermott Classic in 1997. The eighteenth hole at English Turn is among the more difficult finishing holes in golf, particularly for a player seeking to corral that elusive victory. It requires a deep breath and trust in your swing, assuming that it can be trusted under the circumstances.

Part of every professional golfer's pre-shot routine is standing behind his ball, facing his target and visualizing the shot he intends to hit. At English Turn, Faxon attempted to see a long, straight drive that landed in the fairway, but his mind experienced technical difficulties.

"I'm on the tee, and I'm thinking about how I can make a 9 on the last hole," Faxon said. "I've got a four-shot lead and instead of aiming right down the middle, I said, 'OK, start this over land.' And then I hit it into a bunker, and now I'm thinking, 'Oh, if I skull it under the lip I can't get it out, and then I've got a drop in the bunker and it'll be plugged and I can't get that out.' Endless scenarios were going through my brain. But as long as I don't think about it when I'm pulling the trigger, I'm all right."

The demon negative thoughts failed to override his golf swing, however. On the day of reckoning, when hearts beat palpably faster and nerve endings are exposed for the world to see, Faxon stared down the loathsome C word and prevailed.

16

WINNERS AND LOSERS...
THE AFTERMATH

Corey Pavin was on top of the world, which as night fell on June 18, 1995, was the roof of the storied clubhouse at Shinnecock Hills in Southampton, Long Island, New York. By then, tranquillity had returned to this summer playground for the privileged, several hours after Pavin had chased his 4-wood shot up the eighteenth fairway, an attempt to get a better view of a big shot that was about to transform the career of this small man.

He was on the verge of winning the United States Open, among the most cherished prizes in golf. His reward was a place in history as well as the prestigious U.S. Open Championship Cup, a cumbersome piece of hardware, particularly in the hands of a diminutive man.

"I'll tell you one thing," Pavin said, gripping the trophy tightly with both hands, "it's going to be a long time before I let this thing out of my sight."

It was not an idle threat. The celebration party had dwindled to six—Pavin and his wife Shannon, Lee Janzen and his wife Beverly, and Pavin's caddy and his manager. They had scaled the roof of the oldest clubhouse in American golf. They brought with them a supply of champagne and, of course, the U.S. Open Championship Cup, and they sat there in the fading light toasting Pavin's victory and reliving the shots that produced it.

The euphoria experienced by those who win manifests itself in many ways, from quiet reflection to raucous celebration. Those who lose, meanwhile, are left to wonder why. Occasionally per-spective is lost. Sometimes it is found.

Payne Stewart needed virtually a lifetime to finally get it right, as he did at the AT&T Pebble Beach National Pro-Am in the final year of his life. Earlier in his career, he was not necessarily gra-cious, either in victory or in defeat. In defiance of golf etiquette, he was too exuberant a winner when victory came at the expense of another's misfortune at the PGA Championship in 1989. Mike Reid lost a tournament that was his to win, handing it off to a glee-ful recipient, Payne Stewart. When Stewart finished second at Pebble Beach one year, he angrily and wordlessly made straight for his rental car, leaving in his wake a trail of reporters searching only for an explanation.

But now he was forty-two, spiritually transformed, and by all accounts finally having found the requisite maturity to bring his life into balance. Win or lose, Stewart knew what he intended to do the moment the AT&T ended. It offers an eerie reminder of what was lost in that fateful flight that claimed his life several months later. Earlier in the week, he was speaking to his ten-year-old son Aaron, who was home in Florida. Stewart had informed him that he would be home Sunday night.

"What time?" Aaron asked.

"Well, you'll be in bed," Stewart replied.

"Can I come wake you up in the morning?"

"I'd love it."

"So that's the deal," Stewart said. "I'm looking forward to about six-thirty, he's going to come walking in there, 'Knock, knock, you awake?' So it will be great. I'll get up, make breakfast, and take him to school."

Stewart led through three rounds at Pebble Beach and was prepar-ing for the final round, when rain forced its cancellation, making Stewart the champion by default. He then spoke eloquently not of the victory, but of where it fit on his list of priorities in life. His reward, he said, was not another trophy or even the $504,000 he had earned. His reward was that he was going home that night.

"I'm not going to blink and miss my family growing up," Stewart said. "Golf is secondary to my family. If I could never play again, so be it. I don't know that I ever really knew what I wanted. Now I know. I know that I want to watch my family grow up and then I'm going to focus on my golf. When I'm home, I'm going to be a father."

Walter Hagen understood inherently that life was too short and that it was imperative that it be lived accordingly, with an ample supply of fun to counter the requisite work. On or off the course he was a memorable figure. He won eleven major championships, and the art of the celebration was his dominion. When he won the PGA Championship in 1925, he inadvertently entered the wrong guest cottage at Olympia Fields, waking and startling an elderly woman, who nonetheless recovered quickly and offered Hagen a nightcap, requiring in return only that he regale her with the story of how he'd won the tournament.

Hagen set the standard.

Those celebrations involving alcohol run the gamut, from graceful sipping to fraternity-house guzzling. David Duval, for instance, has been known to sip cognac with friends to celebrate a victory—not just any cognac, either. His choice is Louis XIII, at upwards of $100 a shot, $1,500 a bottle. Then there are those who wish to party, Australia's Wayne Riley among them. When Riley won the Portuguese Open in 1996, he addressed the media and spoke eloquently about his reformation, how marriage and father-hood had tempered his wild side. Later on, he was seen walking into the clubhouse bar, trophy in tow, announcing, "Are we going to get drunk, or what?"

Lee Westwood declined to mince words when he was asked once what he would do if he won the British Open. "I'd probably get very, very drunk," he said.

Gabriel Hjertstedt won the Tucson Open, which presents a conquistador's helmet to the winner. He was asked what he intended to do with it. "Maybe fill it with champagne tonight," he said.

In fact, whatever celebrating he intended to do would have to have been done on his flight to Miami later that night. At least he was flying first class. "I actually booked it first class at the start of the week," he said. "Put pressure on myself."

Duffy Waldorf is certain to celebrate with a vintage wine; he has an eighteen-hundred-bottle collection in the cellar of his Santa Clarita, California, home. "I do have a couple of bottles picked out for occasions like this," he said in the aftermath of his victory in the Buick Classic in 1999. "I've got a 1975 French wine."

When Jose Maria Olazabal won his first Masters in 1994, his manager, Sergio Gomez, went to a market and cleaned out the shelves of champagne, only to learn at the checkout line that alcohol is not sold on Sunday in Augusta.

Long after Justin Leonard had received the Claret Jug for his victory in the British Open at Royal Troon, he and Corey Pavin sat on the seventeenth green, where hours earlier Leonard had holed a thirty-foot birdie putt that sealed his victory. They drank beer, ate pizza, and smoked cigars—quintessential American male bonding disguised as a victory celebration.

The celebration in earnest was held when Leonard returned home to Dallas the following day. More than a thousand people, including the legendary Byron Nelson and Dallas's mayor Ron Kirk, gathered at Royal Oaks Country Club, Leonard's home course. Jet lag notwithstanding, Leonard signed autographs and gave an oral recitation of the final round for those in attendance, who also got a firsthand look at the Claret Jug.

The Claret Jug clearly is a hands-on trophy. When Ian Baker-Finch won the British Open in 1991, he returned home to Florida and called on a neighbor, Mark O'Meara.

"I want to show you something," Baker-Finch said, handing the Claret Jug to O'Meara.

"I feel fortunate that I won," Baker-Finch told him, "but I truly believe one of the reasons I won was that I was paired with you in the final round. You made it easier for me to deal with the pressure. Some day, you'll be able to have this experience."

The day arrived in July of 1998, when O'Meara won the British Open in a playoff with Brian Watts. Later that night, a man came in and embraced O'Meara. It was Baker-Finch.

"He was total emotion," O'Meara said. "I mean crying. He was so happy for me. I was kind of taken aback. It was really spectacular. It was something you don't see that much in sports. It was very, very special."

Tom Lehman won the British Open in 1996, gaining possession of the Claret Jug for a year. A few months later, he found the prized trophy behind the couch, where his kids play, and noticed that it had been dented. "That trophy is one hundred twenty-five years old," he told his wife, Melissa. "I have to give it back."

Lehman had it repaired and put it on display at a charitable dinner at the Minneapolis Hilton. When the dinner had concluded, Melissa Lehman gave the Claret Jug to Alissa Herron, sister of PGA Tour player Tim Herron, for safekeeping. Alissa was an employee of Signature Sports, the management firm run by Lehman's brother Jim.

Herron, however, was not going straight home. She, her friends, and the Claret Jug went first to Brit's Pub in downtown Minneapolis. It had just closed, though Herron's group began chanting, "Open up, we got the cup!" Brit's Pub did not reopen, and so the party moved on to The Times, another saloon just down the street. The Times was open. Meanwhile, the bartender who had turned away the crowd at Brit's suspected that the Claret Jug might have been stolen and called the police.

A quick phone call to Lehman revealed that the jug had not

been stolen, and Herron was not arrested. Instead, she and her friends celebrated by drinking shots of Jameson's Irish Whiskey from the Claret Jug.

"That jug has taken some lumps," Lehman said. "The R and A [Royal and Ancient, which conducts the British Open] probably isn't happy. If I win the Open again, they'll probably give me a medal and say, 'We'll keep the trophy.'"

The traditional champion's dinner followed Tiger Woods's historic victory at the Masters in 1997. When Woods arrived in the dining room, the waiters, busboys, and cooks, all of them black, lined up and gave him a sustained ovation. Afterward, Wood returned to the home that he was renting for the week and had a quiet celebration with family and friends, each of whom offered a toast. A few hours later, he repaired to his room and fell asleep, cradling the green jacket.

Lanny Wadkins inadvertently crumpled up his $45,000 winner's check and tossed it into the fireplace during a night of celebrating following his victory in the PGA Championship at Pebble Beach in 1977. Fortunately, the check had missed the flames and Wadkins later discovered it in time to salvage it.

Roger Maltbie was among the few who could relate to this story. In 1975 he won the Pleasant Valley Classic, for which he received a check for $40,000. He stuffed it in a pocket that contained a wad of bills, then went to a bar to celebrate. He pulled the wad of bills from his pocket, tossed it onto the bar, and bought drinks for everyone, himself included, of course.

When he awoke the following morning, "the first thing I wanted to do was buy a paper to read about what a hero I was," he said. He reached in his pocket only to discover that his money and the check were gone. Maltbie had inadvertently tossed the check along with his money onto the bar the night before. The check was found later by a cleaning woman.

One of the more renowned celebrations came hours after Tom

Watson won the British Open at Muirfield in 1980. Champagne was the celebratory drink of choice for Watson, who after dinner noticed Ben Crenshaw and others by the eighteenth green. Crenshaw intended to play the tenth and eighteenth holes with antique clubs and a gutta-percha ball. Watson challenged him to a two-hole match in the twilight and won using a modern ball.

Three years earlier, when Watson beat Jack Nicklaus to win the British Open, he and his wife, Linda, were in their hotel room overlooking the course. Suddenly a Scottish bagpiper began playing and did so for about an hour, raising the hairs on Watson's arms. "It was then," he said, "that I really fell in love with the game."

Crenshaw's own love affair with the game is already well documented. When he won the Masters in 1984, the celebration was relatively subdued. When he finally returned to the home at which he was staying, the Gatlin Brothers were there, ready to commence a celebration. For Crenshaw, for whom golf history is a passion, it was more a time of reflection. After a couple of quick drinks, he went to bed. He returned to his home in Austin, Texas, the next day, watched a videotape of the tournament, and said he cried for four days.

Olin Browne won the Canon Greater Hartford Open in 1998, after which he turned philosophical. "The game teaches you resilience and it teaches you to accept defeat, which is a hard thing for an athlete," he said. "You get hung with a loser moniker, man, it's a hard way to go through life. Think of all the great shots you've hit. If you have one great shot, you have ten mediocre shots and five horrible ones, and the learning process is so demanding and the learning curve so extraordinary. The game humbles people in a hurry.

"It has a way of beating you up, a way of pushing you around. So I'm here in a very humble mode right now, and I'm thanking the golf gods. I'll make the appropriate sacrifices to them this evening."

There are those who lose who deal with their pain in diverse ways, some with humor, others with anger. Larry Mize was the man who lost to Browne in Hartford, tying for second, in part because a wayward 5-iron shot that was an attempt to work back toward the target but clipped a branch and caromed into some trees adjacent to the fifteenth green. "I'm coming back tonight and cutting those branches down," he said.

The star-crossed career of Greg Norman bottomed out at the '96 Masters. For three rounds, it appeared as though Norman would secure the green jacket he so intensely coveted. He began the tournament with a 63 and by Saturday night held a six-stroke lead. It was a safe enough margin that friends at home in Hobe Sound, Florida, began decorating his jet hanger to welcome him home later that night. By the end of the day, after Norman had surrendered the lead and lost the Masters in one of history's more lamentable collapses, they were rushing back to the airport to remove the decorations.

The friends remained behind to welcome him anyway. When he arrived Sunday night, they all sat on his jet, talking and drinking beer until early the next day. The next morning, he awoke angry and hung over, he said. "Monday was tough."

Norman has been on the celebratory end of major championships, too, the first time in 1986, when he won the British Open on the Ailsa Course at Turnberry. Several hours later, what seemed to be a party on the moonlit eighteenth green attracted the attention of a security guard, who went over to investigate. He discovered the newly minted Open champion and friends, enjoying multiple champagne toasts to the victor.

John Cook was on the threshold of winning his first major championship at the British Open in 1999, when his two-and-a-half-foot birdie putt at the seventeenth hole spun out. Still, heading to eighteen, he was a stroke ahead of Nick Faldo, who was playing behind him. Cook then missed the green with his approach at eighteen, leading to a bogey that dropped him into a tie for the lead. When Faldo birdied seventeen and parred eighteen, Cook had lost by a demoralizing stroke.

Traveling home the next day, Cook was a captive audience on his British Airways flight. "They showed highlights of the British Open," he said. "They said, 'England's favorite son captures another Open, unknown American, John who? blows the whole thing.' That was pretty bad."

Tom Lehman, a former British Open champion, in a four-year stretch finished third, second, third, and fifth in the U.S. Open, an impressive run of frustration that threatened to have an enduring impact on him. How, he was asked, was he going to get over the last installment of near misses?

"I have no idea," he said.

"How about," his wife, Melissa, said, according to *Sports Illustrated*, "we go home and have great sex all night?"

"That would work," Lehman replied.

Brandel Chamblee is an engaging, entertaining man who is relatively unknown to those outside the ropes. This cast him as a villain when he and the popular Payne Stewart were vying for the Greater Vancouver Open title in 1998. Chamblee, however, outplayed Stewart head to head in the final round to win.

At the trophy presentation, Chamblee took the microphone and said, "I'd like to thank the people who were pulling for me," he said. "Both of you."

Later on, he found humility a useful tool for describing the perspective the game had taught him.

"Everybody who plays this game is humbled by it, except maybe Tiger Woods," Chamblee said. "Everybody who plays has had a bad stretch. Even when I've played poorly, I've enjoyed it. It's fun to go out and try to figure it out. So really it's like that bumper sticker. A bad day of golf is better than a good day at work."

The late Julius Boros recognized how privileged he was to have played professional tournament golf for a living, the alternative holding no appeal. The alternative is called work. Boros expressed puzzlement once when it was suggested to him that he consider retirement.

"Retire to what?" Boros said, speaking, perhaps, on behalf of several generations of professional golfers. "I'm a golfer and a fisherman. There's no place to retire to."